# Capturing the Organization Organism

## AN OUTSIDE-IN APPROACH TO ENTERPRISE ARCHITECTURE

John Alexander

Technics Publications
BASKING RIDGE, NEW JERSEY

2 Lindsley Road
Basking Ridge, NJ 07920 USA
https://www.TechnicsPub.com

Cover design by Lorena Molinari

Edited by Lauren McCafferty

First Edition

First Printing 2018

Copyright © 2018 John Alexander

| ISBN, print ed. | 9781634624138 |
| ISBN, Kindle ed. | 9781634624145 |
| ISBN, PDF ed. | 9781634624169 |

Library of Congress Control Number: 2018958504

*For FPB, the result of hours of discussion and scribbles on the back of countless beer mats.*

# Acknowledgements

This book has been a long time in the making. It's taken nearly 8 years of writing and re-writing, and much longer than that in gelling out the ideas. Like some of my similar projects, I bounced ideas off many people, too many to list them all here. Thanks go to Graeme Simsion, who taught me so much and led the way, as well as the whole gang at Simsion Bowles and Associates – working with you all was a great pleasure. Particular thanks also go to Andrew Rydlewski, when we both worked at Optus Communications, and who asked the first crucial question which triggered my thinking and, eventually, this book. My thanks also go to Jeyathevan Velupillai at Maxis Communications in Malaysia, and Paul Mazouat at Telcordia Technologies, both of whom gave me projects to do which I didn't think I could do, then trusted me to get on with it, and deliver, which I hope I did. This book has been such a project. Thanks also go to Somchai (Sam) Boonhaicharoen, when we were working together in Bangkok where we tried to code some of this stuff into an all-products ordering and billing system, but ran out of funds, as the project was too big for us. My thanks also go out to my publisher, Steve Hoberman, who is very brave and accepted this book for publication from a first timer. Finally, my thanks to my family, none of whom understood any of this stuff, for their patience, and to my dear late parents who nevertheless supported me with this work.

# Contents

# Introduction

When we set out to do something, especially if it's a major undertaking, we first need to answer some questions:

- **Why?** The answer to this first question is the reason for doing something.

- **What?** Always the second question, the answer to which defines what we will be doing about that particular "something" identified in the first question.

- **How?** Usually the third question, which spells out the method we will be using to do that something. This is the methodology question.

- **When?** How much? How long? Who? These are the questions about managing our initiative. These are project management questions.

- **Where?** Depending on the initiative, this question locates the "what," or may locate the project (in which case it is a project management question).

Developing an information systems enterprise architecture for an organization is a lot of work. There already exists much literature about the "how" question, so this book steers away from methodology as much as possible. The project management-related questions are likewise not within the scope of this book. This book focuses on the "why" and the "what" questions.

The approach taken in this book is to assert that an organization is like a living organism. The internal workings of any living thing must allow that organism to thrive within the environment in which it is operating. These "internal workings" within an organism (including, for example, organs, tissues, and nerves) are analogous to the "information systems" within an organization.

Staying with that analogy, as the environment for the organism changes, the internal mechanisms will have to adapt. For instance, the physical features of domesticated felines have changed and adapted to their housecat lives – you need only compare your cat to a tiger to see that. Similarly, the environment of a business may change over time, with mergers, changes in leadership, new technology, and countless other disruptions. Just like an organism, the business must change and adapt, ensuring that its systems and processes still work in the new environment.

This book uses this analogy as a starting point to discuss the "why" and "what" questions of enterprise architecture, specifically regarding information systems in organizations. To begin this process, we must switch views – from the traditional EA approach of looking only at the internal factors, to a new, holistic view that considers the external environment. In other words, while most EA discussions are "inside-out," in this book, we will attempt to go "outside-in." Of course, in order to find utility in this new viewpoint, we must do a bit more digging.

As such, this book does the following:

- Describes an organizational structure that is common to all organizations, regardless of the enterprise they are involved with.

- Uses data subject areas[1] from one part of EA (the enterprise data model artifact) to describe what is internal and what is external to the organization. Note that this is the only artifact that is actually used in this book.

---

[1] Subject areas are complete data sub-models which relate to the same subject matter. One example is the Product subject area, which contains the detailed data model of the products that the organization provides for its customers.

- Describes connections between what is external and what is internal. This means describing how change is transmitted from external to internal environments, and how that change affects the architecture.

- Defines the enterprise architecture of business functions and/or business application systems that, at a *broad* level, are common to all organizations.

- Describes how, at a more *detailed* level, common business application systems for organizations must be unique, due to the different business environments in which they operate.

- Discusses integration requirements across an organization's business application systems, and how to address these requirements with a disparate COTS-based portfolio, while also exploring the Artificial Intelligence (now commonly known as AI) possibilities of an integrated environment.

- Discusses six key questions to get started understanding the organization and its operating environment, and applies the main points of this book to several non-traditional organizations.

- Provides a high-level map of the organization and the environment in which it operates. This will assist EA practitioners in better understanding the organization, and will empower organizations to better understand themselves.

- Concludes with a summary of the major ideas of the new EA approach.

The intended audience for this book includes *both* information systems enterprise architects and senior non-technical business managers. To make it sensible to both audiences, the book does not stray too far into the technical.

# CHAPTER 1

# About Enterprise Architecture

Enterprise Architecture refers to a set of disciplines within the field of Information and Communications Technology (ICT)[2]. These disciplines attempt to examine an organization's information and communication systems, in order to:

- Understand what the organization requires in the way of ICT infrastructure to operate effectively (the architecture)

- Provide a rational roadmap to the organization to acquire and develop that ICT infrastructure (the ICT strategic plan)

Enterprise Architecture recognizes that data and information are the lifeblood of an organization's ability to operate effectively and efficiently. It also recognizes that the acquisition and effective deployment of the correct ICT infrastructure to collect, store, and provide that data and information can be a costly exercise, which, if not carried out successfully, can lead to endless frustration. In many organizations, the ICT infrastructure not only represents a significant percentage

---

[2] Note the terms ICT (Information and Communications Technology), IT (Information Technology), and IS (Information Systems) are often used interchangeably. IT and ICT both refer to the same things, with ICT including communications technology. The "technology" tends to include both software systems and hardware. In contrast, IS applies only to software and business applications systems, and excludes the technology. For simplicity we use the term "IT" in this book, as it's probably the most commonly used term in computing.

of their total capital investment but is also instrumental in running their business.

Enterprise Architecture studies the organization to provide a rational basis for the acquisition and effective deployment of ICT. The ultimate goal here, of course, is to enable the organization to not simply operate but operate effectively.

A good definition of "Enterprise Architecture" is:

> *An enterprise architecture (EA) is a rigorous description of the structure of an enterprise, which comprise enterprise components (business entities), the externally visible properties of those components, and the relationships (the behavior) between them. EA describes the terminology, the composition of enterprise components, and their relationships with the external environment, and the guiding principles for the requirement, design, and evolution of an enterprise. This description is comprehensive, including enterprise goals, business process, roles, organizational structures, organizational behaviors, business information, software applications and computer systems.[3]*

Evidently, the Enterprise Architecture (EA) looks at and describes the *internal* structure, organization, behavior, and inter-relationships between components of the organization. Although some of the descriptions also describe the way components interact with the external environment and external objects, traditional EA still focuses on the internals of an organization.

In this context, an "organization" or "enterprise" can be defined as:

> *…a complex, socio-technical system that comprises interdependent resources of people, information, and technology that must interact with each other and their environment in support of a common mission.[4]*

---

[3] Wikipedia: https://bit.ly/2LgOSyl.

[4] Ibid.

An organization usually describes its EA in terms of lists, documents, drawings, and models, together called *artifacts*. These artifacts are produced using several sophisticated analytical tools and techniques.

Techniques include models about different aspects of the business such as activity process flows, models of the data of interest, scenarios (e.g. Use Cases) that the business wants supported in the proposed system. Together, these comprise the "artifacts" used in EA, as well as in designing individual business application systems. Software tools are often used to draw up and document these models. These tools can range from simple drawing applications to complete code generation systems, and are sometimes referred to as CASE (computer aided/assisted software engineering) tools.

These tools and techniques have been rapidly evolving, especially in the last 25 years. Practitioners of EA are often called Enterprise Architects, and they are very skilled at using this technology. Thus, the UK National Computing Centre EA best practice guidance states:

> *Normally an EA takes the form of a comprehensive set of cohesive models that describe the structure and functions of an enterprise. …. The individual models in an EA are arranged in a logical manner that provides an ever-increasing level of detail about the enterprise: its objectives and goals; its processes and organization; its systems and data; the technology used and any other relevant spheres of interest.[5]*

This definition certainly applies to two of the major traditional EA frameworks – Zachman and TOGAF. Other EA frameworks that have evolved in recent years also tend to take this approach, including the United States Department of Defense Architecture Framework (DoDAF), the United Kingdom Ministry of Defense Architecture Framework (MODAF), the NATO Architecture Framework (NAF), and others. DoDAF v1.5 takes these framework models further by defining *views* (including the overarching All View, the Operational View, the Systems View, and the Technical Standards View), which depict

---

[5] Ibid.

perspectives of an architecture. Note that the use of views or perspectives (also called *domains*) through an EA is not new; in fact, it is a core component of Zachman and TOGAF. We shall have a quick look at Zachman and TOGAF in the next section.

Enterprise architecture frameworks focus on "what" to cover in an EA, and how these areas of interest are linked. The methodologies or techniques used to model the enterprise, the "how," is not relevant. Whether an EA practitioner chooses to use one of the variations of the object methods, or a more traditional Information Engineering approach, is outside the scope of this discussion.

## Traditional approaches

The Zachman Framework for Enterprise Architecture (sometimes abbreviated to simply "Zachman"), and The Open Group Architecture Framework (usually known by its abbreviation TOGAF), are two of the most ubiquitous EA frameworks used today. Even some of the other EA frameworks mentioned above share many of their concepts with these two frameworks. It is therefore important that we should take a quick (i.e., not exhaustive) look at these two frameworks before proceeding further.

### Zachman Framework

The Zachman Framework for Enterprise Architecture provides a formal and structured way of viewing and defining an enterprise, using a two dimensional matrix based on the intersection of six questions (What, Where, When, Why, Who, How) and six rows or transformations, one for each view (Contextual, Conceptual, Logical, Physical, Detailed, and the bottom row, not used in EA, of the Functioning Enterprise). John Zachman first developed the framework in the 1980s while working at IBM and has since updated it several times.

The current high-level view of the Zachman Framework (i.e., the top 5 rows) is shown in Figure 1.[6]

Figure 1: A summary of the Zachman Framework.

| | Why | How | What | Who | Where | When |
|---|---|---|---|---|---|---|
| **Contextual** | Goal List | Process List | Material List | Organizational Unit & Role List | Geographical Locations List | Event List |
| **Conceptual** | Goal Relationship | Process Model | Entity Relationship Model | Organizational Unit & Role Rel. Model | Locations Model | Event Model |
| **Logical** | Rules Diagram | Process Diagram | Data Model Diagram | Role relationship Diagram | Locations Diagram | Event Diagram |
| **Physical** | Rules Specification | Process Function Specification | Data Entity Specification | Role Specification | Location Specification | Event Specification |
| **Detailed** | Rules Details | Process Details | Data Details | Role Details | Location details | Event Details |

The Zachman Framework is a taxonomy for organizing architectural artifacts (including models, descriptions, specifications, or documentation). The rows describe the artifacts' targets (i.e. the view, perspective, or domain that the artifacts describe), while the columns indicate the issue or context. Each cell within the matrix defines a particular type of model or architectural artifact.

---

6    Note that the three diagrams in this discussion of the Zachman Framework, shown in figures 1, 2, and 3, have been reproduced from the Wikipedia article found at https://en.wikipedia.org/wiki/Zachman_Framework. As far as the author is aware, these diagrams are in the public domain, and have been used for descriptive purposes only, as is the brief discussion in this sub-section , which is also based on that article. Readers who wish to further explore the Zachman Framework should refer to the original publications by Dr. John Zachman.

Figure 2 gives the row definitions; the columns in Figure 2 are ordered differently from those in Figure 1. There is no significance to the order of the columns within the Zachman Framework. Note also that Figure 2 contains the sixth row, Functioning Enterprise, which came as a later development of the Framework.

Figure 2: A description of the rows in the Zachman Framework.

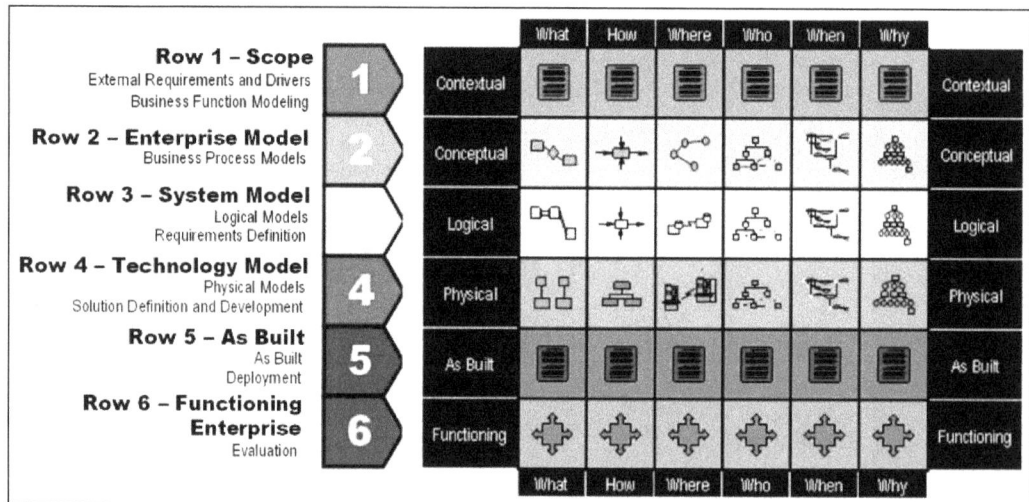

Each row perspective focuses on the fundamental questions asked in each column, answering those questions from that perspective using models. Thus, all models are consistent vertically, providing the answer for each view in each row, and answering all the questions at that view level across the whole row, using different models for each question. The questions asked (in no particular order) are:

- The data description – What?
- The function description – How?
- The network description – Where?
- The people description – Who?
- The time description – When?
- The motivation description – Why?

What makes Zachman's Framework useful is that each element on either axis of the matrix is distinguishable from all the other elements on that axis. The models in each cell of the matrix are not successive levels of increasing detail going down the column but are different representations, based on the view that they serve in each row.

The focus for each cell in this framework (by row then column) is:

## Contextual

- *Why* – Goal List – primary high-level organizational goals

- *How* – Process List – list of all known processes

- *What* – Material List – list of all known organizational entities

- *Who* – Organizational Unit and Role List – list of all organization units, sub-units, and identified roles

- *Where* – Geographical Locations List – locations important to organization; can be large and small

- *When* – Event List – list of triggers and cycles important to organization

## Conceptual

- *Why* – Goal Relationship Model – identifies hierarchy of goals that support primary goals

- *How* – Process Model – provides process descriptions, input processes, output processes

- *What* – Entity Relationship Model – identifies and describes the organizational materials and their relationships

- *Who* – Organizational Unit and Role Relationship Model – identifies enterprise roles and units and the relationships between them

- *Where* – Locations Model – identifies enterprise locations and the relationships between them

- *When* – Event Model – identifies and describes events and cycles related by time

## Logical

- *Why* – Rules Diagram – identifies and describes rules that apply constraints to processes and entities without regard to physical or technical implementation

- *How* – Process Diagram – identifies and describes process transitions expressed as verb-noun phrases without regard to physical or technical implementation

- *What* – Data Model Diagram – identifies and describes entities and their relationships without regard to physical or technical implementation

- *Who* – Role Relationship Diagram – identifies and describes roles and their relations to other roles by types of deliverables without regard to physical or technical implementation

- *Where* – Locations Diagram – identifies and describes locations used to access, manipulate, and transfer entities and processes without regard to physical or technical implementation

- *When* – Event Diagram – identifies and describes events related to each other in sequence, cycles occur within and between events, without regard to physical or technical implementation

## Physical

- *Why* – Rules Specification – expressed in a formal language; consists of rule name and structured logic to specify and test rule state

- *How* – Process Function Specification – expressed in a technology specific language, hierarchical process elements are related by process calls

- *What* – Data Entity Specification – expresses relationships in a technology-specific format; each entity is defined by name, description, and attributes

- *Who* – Role Specification – expresses roles performing work and workflow components at the work product detailed specification level

- *Where* – Location Specification – expresses the physical infrastructure components and their connections

- *When* – Event Specification – expresses transformations of event states of interest to the enterprise

## Detailed Representation

The cells with the detailed representation show and describe the physical implementation of the Rules (Why), Process (How), Data (What), Roles (Who), Locations (Where), and Events (When).

The Zachman Framework includes a set of rules, depicted in Figure 3. These rules tell users how to use the framework, and how it works.

For a useful EA, it is not necessary to complete every cell in detail. There is flexibility in the detail that an enterprise would find useful to complete. For example, a manufacturer whose business goals focus on process and inventory would find the What, How, and perhaps Where columns of great use, while a travel agency, where the focus on people and events is more important, would find the Who, When and Where columns of greater use. The Why column should always be present, as this provides the business drivers for all the other columns.

Figure 3: Key rules of the Zachman Framework.

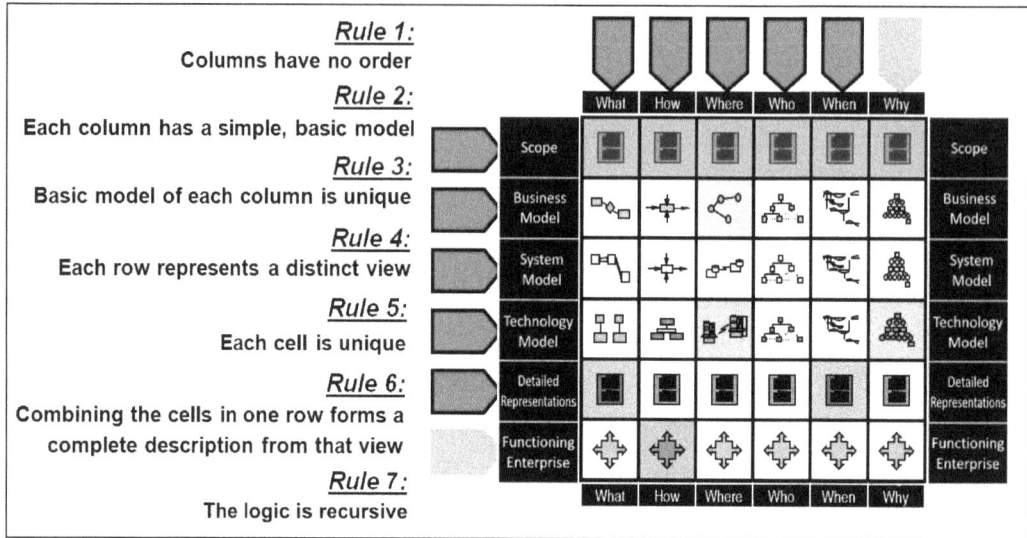

Imagine, for example, a solution architect were to commence a project designing and developing a point IT solution (i.e. an IT solution addressing a single or limited set of needs for an organization), using artifacts in the Logical row. They might consider developing at least outline models for the Contextual and Conceptual rows, if these did not already exist. This would provide scope, context, and a much better understanding of where the proposed point solution fits, in relationship with other existing IT solutions and, most importantly, the business of the organization. This is especially the case where nowadays it is rare that a point IT solution is a standalone solution which does not need interfaces and integration with other existing or planned point IT solutions.

The "Why" column of the Zachman Framework, as mentioned above, focuses on:

- At the Contextual row – organizational Goals

- At the Conceptual row – Goal relationships and hierarchies of goals (e.g. goals supporting other goals)

- At the Logical row – Rules that apply constraints to processes and entities

- At the Physical row – Rules specification, in formal language and logic

This book attempts to add value to and complement these questions (especially the "Why" column) by considering the organization's environment, using an outside-in approach.

## TOGAF

The Open Group Architecture Framework (TOGAF) is a framework that provides a comprehensive approach to the design, planning, implementation, and governance of an enterprise information architecture.[7] TOGAF takes a high-level and holistic approach to design, and is typically modeled at four levels: Business, Application, Data, and Technology. TOGAF comprises a set of tools that can be used for developing a broad range of different architectures. TOGAF provides all of the following:

- A method for defining an information system in terms of a set of building blocks

- A map to show how the building blocks fit together

- A set of standard tools

- A common vocabulary

- A list of recommended standards

- A list of compliant products that can be used to implement the building blocks

---

[7] Wikipedia: https://bit.ly/2NWr69k.

TOGAF was developed by the Architecture Forum of The Open Group, released in 1995, and has continuously evolved since then. The latest version, launched in February of 2009, is TOGAF 9. Figure 4[8] provides an overview of the TOGAF Architecture Development Method (ADM).

Unlike the Zachman Framework, TOGAF is both an architecture framework and a methodology for developing an EA.

The architecture framework of TOGAF is based on four domains, namely:

- **Business Architecture** (or business process architecture), which defines the business strategy, governance, organization, and key business processes of the organization.

- **Applications Architecture**, which provides a blueprint for the individual application systems to be deployed, the interactions between the application systems, and their relationships to the core business processes of the organization with the frameworks for services to be exposed as business functions for integration.

- **Data Architecture**, which describes the structure of an organization's logical and physical data assets and the associated data management resources.

- **Technical (or Technology) Architecture**, which describes the hardware, software and network infrastructure needed to support the deployment of core, mission-critical applications.

---

[8]   Note that Figure 4 has been reproduced from the Wikipedia article named in the previous footnote. As far as the author is aware, this diagram is in the public domain, and is reproduced here to assist the brief description in the text of this sub-section, also based on that article, but which is not intended to be a full discussion of TOGAF. Readers who wish to further explore TOGAF should refer to the original publications.

Figure 4: The TOGAF Architecture Development Method.

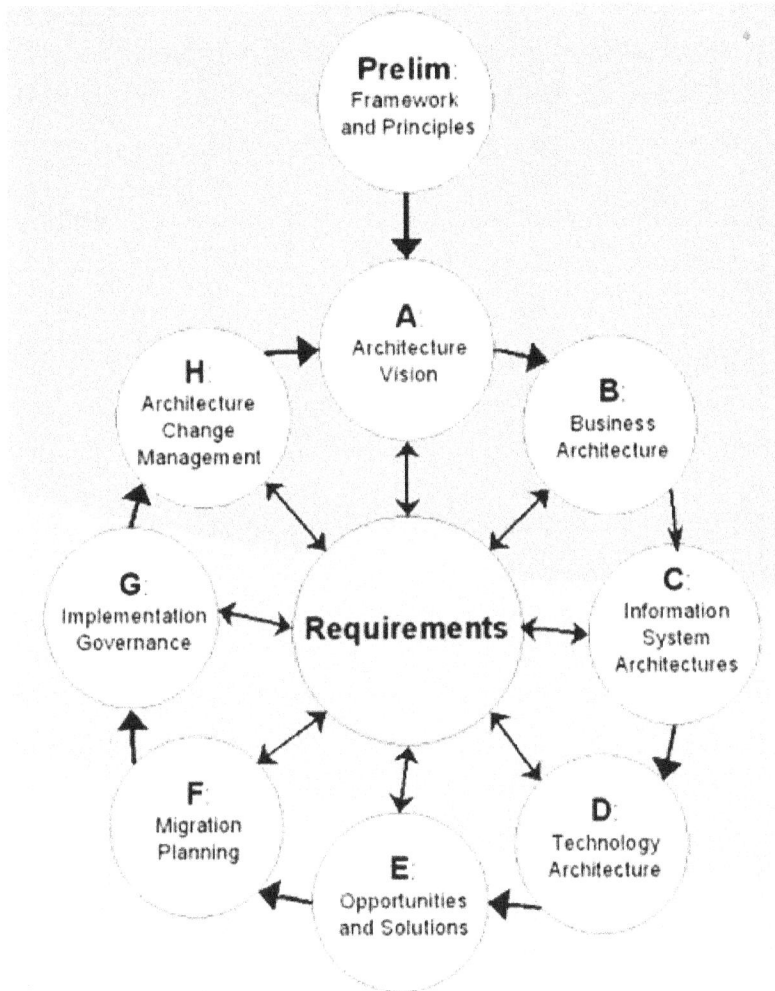

The methodology is called the Architecture Development Method (ADM) which specifies the approach to be applied when developing an organization's EA. ADM, which is tailorable to an organization's needs, is employed to manage the execution of architecture planning activities. The process is cyclic and often used iteratively. Each step requires a check with the Requirements.

One might consider the Enterprise Continuum like a "virtual repository" (or, in the words of TOGAF 9, a "real repository") of all the architecture assets available to an organization. These include architectural models, patterns, descriptions, and other artifacts. These artifacts may exist within the enterprise and in the IT industry at large.

The Enterprise Continuum consists of both the Architecture Continuum and the Solutions Continuum. The Architecture Continuum specifies the structuring of reusable architecture assets, and includes rules, representations, and relationships of the information system(s) available to the enterprise. The Solutions Continuum describes the implementation of the Architecture Continuum by defining reusable solutions as building blocks.

Many CASE (computer assisted/aided software engineering) tools have been certified to at least TOGAF 8, including IBM's Rational System Architect (version 10 or later) and Sparx Systems' Enterprise Architect.

TOGAF is derived partly from an earlier incarnation of DoDAF, called TAFIM (Technical Architecture Framework for Information Management), developed by the US government. In turn, some other EA frameworks are based on or derived from TOGAF. For example, the SAP Enterprise Architecture Framework is an extension of TOGAF, designed to better support commercial off-the-shelf (COTS) products and Service-Oriented Architecture (SOA).

With the Business Architecture domain, TOGAF shares many similar concepts to the Contextual top row within the Zachman Framework. For example:

- Business process is analogous to Zachman's "How"

- Business strategy is analogous to Zachman's "Why"

- Business governance and organization analogous to Zachman "Who," and possibly "Where"

As with the Zachman Framework, this book attempts to add value to, and complement, mainly the TOGAF Business Architecture domain, by considering the organization's environment and its effects on the EA, through using an outside-in approach.

## Issues with traditional approaches

It was the unique challenges of the Information Technology (IT) world that drove the development of traditional Enterprise Architectures (EAs). These challenges led to the following objectives for EAs:

- Understanding and making sense of the business that IT supports

- Maximizing the cost-effectiveness of an organization's IT investment

- Understanding and solving the integration challenges between new and legacy IT solutions

- Predicting where IT can or should be developed to support and enable business

However, IT isn't the only ones who use EA to better understand the business it serves. Business architects also use EA to improve the effectiveness and efficiency of the business; specifically, to:

- Propose innovations in the organization and/or structure of the business

- Centralize or federate business processes

- Improve the quality or timeliness of business information

- Justify money spent on IT

As such, the primary emphasis has been on the internals of the business. This is similar to taking an MRI scan of a living organism, to see where all the parts are and how they operate and fit together, but ignoring how the organism operates in its environment. In addition, understand the:

- Current business process – including alterations to those processes due to applying Business Process Re-engineering (BPR). Use of BPR is usually driven by the need for greater efficiencies, or changes as a result of IT taking on part or all of the business process.

- Current business goals and strategies – these are accepted as they are, with little or no analysis of their context.

- Current business rules – again, these are accepted as given, with little or no analysis of context.

The idea that developing an EA for an organization can provide predictive capabilities, business efficiencies, and business effectiveness with respect to IT investment and deployment, is one of the core ambitions of the EA disciplines. However, because EA currently looks almost exclusively at the internals of an organization, it is almost bound to fail in its predictive ambitions. Why is this so?

To understand this major inability of current EA frameworks to be predictive, we will use a simple analogy. If you want to understand how a cat works, you must open it up and look inside. You will get a great view of its internal organs, skeleton, and what it ate for breakfast. This method of examining how the cat works will provide us with a splendid description of its anatomy, structure, internal processes, and interdependencies between different parts and systems, rules about timing of events between the parts, and reactions to those events by each part. However, none of this examination of the internal workings of the cat will tell us anything much about the environment that the cat must operate in, what it contributes to that environment, and what it takes out of that environment. Nor will it tell us very much about its behavior in that environment, or why it behaves the way it does.

As with the cat, so it is with organizations and current EA frameworks and approaches. Current EA will provide a splendid and detailed picture of the anatomy, processes, chemistry, and physiology of organizations. In current EA approaches we even ask what the organizational goals and objectives are, what its strategies are, and what rules it operates under. However, current EA tells us little about the environment the organization must operate in, its behavior in that environment, and what it takes out of or puts into that environment. As such, we have little predictive ability to change things, whether to operate more efficiently under the current environment or to respond to changes in that environment. We have insufficient data to make changes. We must guess and assume, and changes made on guesses and assumptions can go wildly (and expensively) wrong.

For EA to be an effective exercise and tool in prediction, managing change, and re-engineering the organization for change, we need to not only know about the anatomy of the organization, we need to observe and get facts about the environment that the organization has to operate in, its current behavior with respect to that environment, and what is likely to change and how that will impact behavior, as well as what is likely to be impacted internally.

In other words, we must treat the organization as an organism operating within an environment. We must study that organism within its environment, its behavior, its outputs to that environment, its inputs from that environment, and its interactions with other organisms.

# CHAPTER 2

# Organization as an Organism

*At the heart of complexity lies simplicity. At the heart of simplicity lies complexity.*

What does it really mean to "treat the organization as an organism operating within an environment?" In this chapter, we will return to the analogy of the cat to help explain this concept, and then use this understanding to explain the concept of the organization as an organism. This will provide a direction to focus on for EA in looking at organizations within their environments.

## Meow

We know certain things about a cat. A cat is a carnivorous animal, which means it must eat meat to survive. Cats do not extract their protein and most other of the nutrients they need to live from vegetable matter. Nor do they prefer carrion (dead or long dead) meat, but prefer their meat freshly killed – usually by themselves. This makes cats hunters.

For this they are admirably adapted, with retractable claws, soft padded feet, fearsome carnivore teeth, and extremely sensitive sensors in the form of vision, hearing, and smell. Some even have fur colors which provide good camouflage.

A cat's mother teaches it behaviors, such as stalking, which make it an effective and successful hunter of other less fortunate animal prey.

Hunting, killing, and eating small animals is what a cat (in the wild) takes from its environment, and uses as input for its own survival. As output back to its environment, a cat in the wild provides a culling service to keep numbers of other animals (such as mice) under control. This service is an important natural stabilizer to the environment, as population explosions would create pest issues if it did not exist. By the same token, if there weren't enough mice, there would be fewer cats – but we will discuss this later.

Through this analogy, we have now established three major principles:

- The organism provides something (a culling service) to its environment, as part of its interaction with that environment.

- The organism uses something (mice) from its environment, as input to its survival. The organism uses these inputs to provide its outputs, and to enable the organism to continue its existence.

- The organism operates in, and interacts with, its environment. This interaction may be in the form of compliance to pre-existing conditions, such as to grow a fur coat to protect the cat against the cold, or other interactions such as finding a living space to bring up its young.

The cat, like most other organisms, also faces direct and indirect competition, within its patch of the environment. Such competition appears in the forms of:

- Competition for input (food) sources. This may be in the form of other cats, or other types of carnivorous animals, such as hawks, which also eat mice.

- Competition for output (culling) services. This may be in the form of too many carnivores, like cats and hawks, leading to a smaller "market" for culling services, as the culled disappear.

- Competition for other required environmental resources. This may be in the form of living space for raising litters of young cats, or for shared resources, such as water sources.

Natural selection through competition has evolved a cat into a successful predator that thrives in its given environment. Should environmental factors change, the cat will need to change – or die out.

Studying the environment and behavior of the organism will provide us with a much better predictive capability for when things change. For example, how would the cat need to be re-engineered if water suddenly became scarce, but other factors remain the same? We might provide a better answer to this question if we had knowledge of both the organism's environment and behavior, as well as the organism's anatomy and internal workings. But with knowledge only of the organism's internal workings, the answer would be pure guesswork.

## Outputs and inputs

When looking at an organization as an organism which operates within its environment, we will use the three major principles established above in the analogy of the cat. These are:

- The organization provides one or more outputs to its environment. We shall call these outputs the organization's *products.*

- The organization takes input from its environment. This input enables the organization to produce its products, and to survive as an organization. We shall call these inputs the organization's *supplies.*

- The organization needs to interact with its environment. This may be in the form of compliance to regulatory requirements, or interacting with regulators to influence legal changes, or working to establish a customer base for its products.

As we shall see, the major interactions that an organization has with its environment are through its products, customers for those products, and supplies it uses, as well as the suppliers for those supplies. We will look at each of these three in detail in the following sub-sections.

## Outputs

Every organization exists to provide products. In this book we define a "product" as:

*Anything (tangible object or intangibles such as information) or service (activity) that is supplied by one entity to meet a want or need by another entity.*

From the above definition, the existence of products implies that there needs to be at least one *customer*, and usually multiple customers, that consume those products. Thus, a product is not a product unless there is, has been, or will be, a customer (i.e. consumer) for that product. Therefore, a product requires a customer – this is one case where one object always requires another object. Practically speaking, the existence of a product guarantees the existence of a customer (either present, past, or future). However, the reverse may not necessarily be true. The existence of a customer does not guarantee the existence of a product.

Remember that a service is included within the definition of (and is a type of) product. The cat from our earlier analogy provides a population control service. In this case, the "customer" is the environment itself. Examples abound of services as products – lawyers and doctors provide professional services to their customers or clients, on a fee-for-service basis – these products consist only of services. However, a service may also be included with an object to provide a complete product package. An example of this is where installation activities (a service) for a product is required, as is the case for some broadband or leased-line connections. The concept of product *packaging* is discussed below.

In the context of EA and this book, it is irrelevant whether the organization provides the product to the customer free of charge, or for a price. There is *always* a price for a product, but that price may not be paid directly by the customer. For example, a volunteer society providing food aid (its product) to impoverished people (its customers) in poor countries still requires funding, in the form of grants or donations. On the other hand, the defense department of a government provides a protection service product for the whole population, who are its customers, and who pay for this service product directly through their taxes.

Products may be included with other products to form a *product package*. In fact, product packages are more common than a single item or service. Even the purchase of a washing machine for example, usually includes a delivery service, an installation service, and a warranty. Products can be tangible things (like a car), intangible things (such as a service or an insurance policy), or a mixture of both, as per the aforesaid example of the delivery and installation of a washing machine (i.e. physical item is the washing machine + service item is the delivery + service item is the installation = complete product package).

In my experience, some organizations have problems classifying and defining what their products are, and what each product package includes. Development of an EA which tries to define the organization's products, may lead to conflicts in the definition of "product" from different parts of the organization.

Customers consume the products an organization provides to them. As mentioned, a customer may not necessarily pay money for the product – the product may be provided "free of charge" to a customer. (Of course, the costs of providing the product are often covered in some other way, like an inconspicuous "service fee"). The term "customer," as used in this book, includes "client" (usually applied to customers of service products), and "stakeholder" (the term substituted for customer by certain organizations to remove possible commercial connotations).

It is useful to group customers into *markets,* which can be further sub-grouped into *market segments*. This kind of grouping is common practice for commercial organizations, and even some non-commercial ones like the division of its "customers" into different levels of need by a food aid voluntary organization. Grouping provides the organization with information about the customer, such as the customer's preferences, the types of products they are interested in, and the segment of the environment in which the organization must operate in with its product/s.

Some organizations even classify those who do not, or have never, obtained a product from that organization as "potential" or "suspect" customers. These organizations or individuals could become customers, given the right conditions (such as the right product package at the right price). Usually these additional classifications of "customer" originate in the marketing sections of organizations. In some organizations, this may lead to a conflict of definition of what is a customer. EA practitioners should be aware of such potential conflicts of definition for both customer and product.

Finally, consider that one organization's output likely serves as another organization's input. For example, a mining operation's output (iron ore) might be used by a steel manufacturer to produce its own output (steel). In turn, this steel could be bought and used as input by a vehicle manufacturing company in order to produce their car products. This series of inputs is called a *supply chain*, and the logistics involved with the supply chain are also important considerations in the environment, which in turn is important and pertinent in developing an EA for any of these organizations.

We shall see later that products, customers, and markets are not the only external factors in the environment. However, they are major factors that you must consider as part of any EA.

## Inputs

Organizations take inputs from other organizations (or people) to produce their products. The "person" entity behaves like the "organization" entity in this context, providing their services as a product, and taking compensation (e.g. a salary or benefits) as input. These organizations (or people) are called *input suppliers* (or simply "suppliers") by the organization taking the input. Depending on the products they produce, or type of organization, inputs may vary. Some examples include:

- A vehicle manufacturer would usually take semi-finished sheet and other metal forms from a steel manufacturer, add components and paint from other manufacturers, and use all these to build completed cars, trucks and other types of vehicles.

- A bank or financial institution would "buy" money from depositors, and "sell" that money as loan and credit products to customers. The "price" of buying this money is paid as interest to depositors; while the "price" of selling this money is paid to the bank as interest by the customers of their loan and credit products. The difference in interest paid out and interest paid in is the bank's margin, which eventually goes towards its profit.

- A legal firm would use input from its lawyers to provide service products to its customers. Such services are typically billed according to time and materials used, the time billing usually being a multiple of the amount paid to the personnel involved in the service, e.g. 3.5 times the individual lawyer's hourly salary rate. The difference is the legal firm's margin on the service products. Note that although some law firms bill on a different basis such as a percentage of damages won, that amount would still need to be a multiple of their input costs.

- Virtually all organizations also have other inputs that they need to produce their outputs. Such inputs include resources they own such as business premises, computing equipment, machine tools, and vehicles, as well as other inputs required to run their business such as utilities used, and administration and managerial effort expended. Such inputs do come at a cost, which is usually factored into the price as an *indirect cost*.

*Inputs* are what an organization uses to produce its **outputs**. Inputs can include outputs (products) from other organizations or services from individuals within the organization, as well as *resources* it owns or uses (including leased resources), such as machinery, vehicles, and premises.

Note that in this book the term "resource" specifically excludes people working for, or on behalf of, an organization. Of course, this is an artificial exclusion, in that the people working for an organization provide the organization's most important inputs. However, we make this exclusion for two basic reasons. Firstly, it simplifies the discussion of EA, and focuses that discussion on the organization, simplifying scope. Secondly, people are not equivalent to other types of resources (such as machines), and should not be treated as such. It is *people* who make things happen in an organization, not the tools.

Also note the similarity between organizations and individuals: individuals provide their services in the form of skills and effort as their service products, utilizing inputs such as salary, other products like food, and resources such as household premises (somewhere to live), a car, and their education (a service product provided to them earlier in life).

## Environmental interactions

Apart from inputs and outputs (i.e. customers, products and suppliers), there are three major types of interactions an organization might have with its environment: events, business arrangements, and locations. We'll describe each briefly here.

An **event** is defined as anything which happens, which is outside of the organization's control, and to which the organization must respond with some activity (or series of activities, as in a process). One common example of an event is an order by a customer for one or more of the organization's products. In the same vein, a payment by a customer is also an event. A less common example of an event is a lightning strike which damages network equipment belonging to a telecommunications organization. Our final example is one you hope to never encounter: an illegal act by one or more of the organization's personnel.

All of these are examples of events that could transpire, and to which an organization must respond with some kind of activity or process. Some events are also triggered by activities – either undertaken by others or by the organization itself. The organization may also undertake activities to avoid triggering events, or at least reduce the probability of an event occurring. We will discuss events in detail later.

A **business arrangement** is any agreement, contract, law, or similar formal or informal device, that guides or defines the behavior of an organization – that is, what the organization does. One common example of a business arrangement is a contract entered with another organization for the supply of products. Another common example is the requirement for an organization listed on the stock exchange to report its performance and plans on a regular basis.

In guiding the behavior of an organization, a business arrangement may force the inclusion or exclusion of certain products into, or from a product package. One example of this was mentioned earlier – that of the inclusion of a warranty, which is the promise of specified action should a product be defective or fail. Finally, an often-overlooked business arrangement is the standard. Standards can play an important part in the behavior of organizations, either because they hold formal certifications under certain international standards such as the ISO 9000 series, or in standards and associated technology which emerge based on a need for commonality/interoperability such as barcoding. Standards also can play an important role in the organization's products, and flow on to its suppliers' products incorporated into its own.

Business Arrangements are relevant to all organizations and are important components of an organization's interaction with its environment. Changes in business arrangements also represent a substantial proportion of environmental changes to which organizations must respond.

A **location**, unlike the first two intangible ideas, is a place in three-dimensional space.[9] Superficially, location seems to be a part of the organization's external environment, but in EA terms, it is not necessarily obvious as to why this is so. One example is the physical location of the organization, and how this affects its customer base, product distribution, and input supply chain.

Changes in any of the organization's supplier or customer locations could affect both the organization's market base and/or its supply chain logistics. A less obvious example is where the customer base is expanded through the inclusion

---

[9] In this book, we will exclude network addresses as locations.

of "potential" customers. These could be located anywhere far from the organization's own outlets or branches. This situation could require internal changes. For example, the establishment of an online store using the Web, plus a supply chain for delivery of products. Such remote sales would also bring into consideration Business Arrangements in other countries (consumer laws and taxes), and is an important consideration for EA.

Again, this section has merely provided an introductory summary of these important factors in an organization's environment. We will discuss each of these in greater detail in later chapters.

## Competition

Competition is a contest between organizations for limited customers or input requirements. There are generally three levels of economic competition, namely:

- Direct competition, where two or more organizations' products perform the same function and are in a contest for the same customers (market).

- Indirect competition, where two or more organizations' products are not the same, but could be substituted for one another. As such, the organizations may compete for a similar set of customers.

- Budget competition, where the customer has available funds to spend on a range of products; the contest between organizations is focused on obtaining the largest share of those funds by sales of their products.

Input (resources) competition is another form of contest between organizations. Input competition involves organizations competing for the input they require to produce their products. This input may vary, depending on the type of organization. One example is that of financial institutions, where there is competition for the investor funds they require for their loan or credit products. Another example is the competition between steelmaking organizations for raw materials, such as iron ore and coal, needed for their refined products.

Competition is a major factor involved in an organization's interaction with its environment, but not the only one. Furthermore, competition may not be limited to the organization's external environment. Some organizations promote internal competition between different parts of the same organization.

---

# Feedback loop

Information back into the organization about its environment including the performance of its products, customer preferences for similar products, volumes and value of sales, and sale prices of equivalent inputs for both the organization and its competitors, forms the feedback which the organization requires to judge its performance and effectiveness, and to adjust its behavior accordingly. This feedback enables organizations to continuously adjust and refine their interactions with their environment, as well as their internal structures and processes. As such, any organization developing an EA must carefully consider these feedback loops.

The feedback generated in these loops is almost always information. Information consists of data structured to provide meaning, as well as unstructured data (such as comments made by individuals). Structured data, as long as it is complete, comprehensive, and precisely structured, provides the most *objective* and comprehensive information for feedback. On the other hand, unstructured data is almost always *subjective*, selective, and anecdotal, if not completely apocryphal (of dubious veracity). However, given the explosion in the use of social media in recent years, unstructured data provides more rapid feedback than structured data, even if it may be less accurate and less objective.

To better understand this difference between immediate unstructured data and delayed structured data, consider the following analogy. Suppose you are walking barefooted through a dark room, and you suddenly step on something unexpected on the floor; the mysterious object is soft, furry, and moved under your foot when you stepped on it. Based on those immediate sensory inputs from your foot, your brain might infer that you stepped on a mouse, rat, or some other unwelcome roommate. As such, your instinctive reaction would probably be to immediately jump away. This reaction is natural, built into our instincts, and could surely come in handy as a survival mechanism if you had stepped on something dangerous.

But what if you had been able to delay that reaction until you gathered more structured data? For instance, you might instead reach for a nearby lamp to shed some light on the situation. In that case, you might see that what you actually stepped on was your dog's furry toy. This delayed but structured data would tell you that you're not in danger. As such, you might change your course of action, from an initial instinct to leap dramatically away, to a more rational response, like using your foot to push the toy aside.

In summary, the information organizations receive back from their environments, in the form of structured and unstructured data, allows the organization to react and adjust its behavior, with respect to that environment. At the same time, the reaction of the organization can be quite different, depending on the type of data which it collects from its environment. We will discuss information, and its importance and relevance to EA, in more detail later in this book.

# CHAPTER 3

# Basic Concepts – What is DONE

In the previous chapter we introduced the concept of organizations as organisms operating within (and interacting with) their environment. In the following section, we will introduce some key factors that form the basis of that interaction.

*Products* are the main outputs from the organization, and the reason for the organization's existence. In turn, products provide the means for the organization to operate successfully in its environment. Products are provided to customers at a cost, regardless of whether that cost is paid by the customer (or "end user").

Products, of course, imply *customers* for those products. Organizations exist because of their customers, and their customers' requirement for their products. Customers can be grouped (or segmented) into markets – those customers which share something in common, and to which certain products can be directed. Customers are usually defined as the end-users of the products, although this definition may vary between and within certain organizations.

*Suppliers* are organizations or individuals who supply an organization with the things it needs to make products. We could expand this definition to include individuals working within the organization (who supply their skill as input to the organization's products, especially in highly specialized service-based organizations, like legal firms). However, for the purposes of this book, we will not extend this definition to include internal workers, but stay with the more limited definition of suppliers being *external* providers to the organization.

Supplier terminology can vary widely. It is not uncommon for enterprise data architects to model both customers and suppliers (and also individuals within organizations) as the same type of entity, called the "Party." This way, the actual role of the party (for instance, as customer or supplier) is modeled separately. This provides many advantages, not least of which any single occurrence of an organization or individual appears once only, but that entity can have multiple roles. This provides a much richer picture of reality.

The next important factor to discuss is *resources*. These are the things which the organization uses, directly or indirectly, to make and deliver its products. Note that resources are *things*; individual persons are excluded. There are many examples of resources, including the organization's premises, computers, machine tools, vehicles, or anything at all that the organization needs to operate in its environment.

An *event* is anything that happens outside of the organization's control, and to which an organization must respond with some kind of activity (or series of activities, as in a process). Events can be as diverse as a lightning strike on network-sensitive equipment (in the example of a telecoms company), a customer order for products, a complaint, or a law suit against the organization.

Events are things that happen which impact the organization – usually from the external environment, but events may also occur internally within the organization. Events may trigger activities, and, in turn, activities can trigger events. Activities may also be undertaken to either increase of decrease the *probability* of an event occurring.

*Activities*, then, are those things that the organization does, usually in response to events (internal or external). A series of linked, planned, and structured, activities is usually known as a *process* or *business process*. Business processes have traditionally been key platforms for analysis in EA. All business processes start with a trigger event. However, activities can trigger events, so the two concepts interact. Also, some activities may aim to avoid certain negative events, such as risk management activities.

*Business Arrangements* are any formal or informal devices, such as agreements, standards, or laws, which guide or control an organization's behavior. Business arrangements influence organizations' behaviors in a variety of ways, from outlawing certain products, through influencing pricing and quality of products, to guiding behavior of employees of the organization. Changes to business arrangements are often drivers to internal organizational changes and external environmental behavior changes.

*Locations* are places in three-dimensional space. The physical locations of the organization, as well as the physical locations of its customers and suppliers, are important environmental factors that the organization must deal with. Other important considerations for an EA are whether the organization's business activities are dependent or independent of its customers, suppliers, and the organization's own locations. There are many methods of defining location, including street addresses, postcodes, and other locality identification, or grid references (e.g., latitude and longitude and GPS positions).

*Competition* is a contest between organizations (and others) for customer spend, or for input required for the organization's products. Competition shapes organizational behavior in many ways in terms of the products provided, the sourcing of inputs, the markets chosen, and the treatment of customers. Therefore, you must consider competition as part of the EA. We identified earlier three types of economic competition on the output side, as well as competition on the input side, and internal competition.

Information about the organization's performance within its environment, as well as about its competitors, is vital to the organization's success in its environment. We identified information as structured or unstructured, objective or subjective, and immediate or delayed. Information for the feedback loop is a vital consideration for an EA.

The above major concepts form the basis of our discussion of EA, the organization, and its operations within its environment. Now that we have a grasp of all the important factors, we are prepared to explore in more detail how to apply these ideas to an EA. First, though, we'll consider one more near-universal concept that will prove useful to our discussion: the functional structure of an organization.

## Structure

For almost every organization, you can organize its functions[10] into three "horizontal" layers, plus one "vertical" layer that intersects all three "horizontal" layers, as illustrated in Figure 5.

Figure 5: The "three -plus -one" layered structure can apply to almost any organization.

| Business Management | Customers & Product Sales |
| | Product Development & Product Build |
| | Suppliers & Supplies |

---

[10]  In the context of this book, the term "function" is used to mean "a grouping of associated processes aimed at fulfilling one or a group of associated goals/objectives." As seen before, a "process" is a set of linked activities. Thus a function is a rollup of activities into processes, and processes into functions.

This three-plus-one model fits nearly every type of organization, including:

- Banks, financial institutions, and insurance organizations

- Telecommunications and media organizations

- Manufacturing, mining, and other primary production organizations

- Pure trading companies and trading organizations

- Government departments and organizations; although these organizations often function as monopolies, thus exhibiting different behaviors than competitive commercial organizations

- Medical organizations such as hospitals and clinics

- Voluntary and non-profit organizations

Some of these types of organizations produce objects (such as cars) as products, and others provide services (such as legal or medical) services as products, but the majority provide a combination of both objects and services.

This "three plus one" model is described in greater detail in the following sections.

## Three layers

In the model illustrated in Figure 5, an organization's core functions appear in three horizontal layers, plus one vertical business management layer. The three horizontal layers are business functions addressing:

- Customers and the products which the organization provides to its customers

- The development and building of the organization's products

- The acquisition and operations for acquiring the necessary supplies (inputs) from suppliers for the development and building of the organization's products

As noted earlier, this three-plus-one model applies to both organizations and individuals. However, this book focuses mainly on organizations and EA for organizations.

## Customers and products

These functions deal with the products that an organization provides for its customers, and its interaction with the customer. Here we'll explore several typical functions for commercial organizations.

*Marketing* is the process of performing market research and promoting products to enhance sales. Market research is determining which products customers want, usually divided into customer categories, each of which form a market segment within the overall market. Marketing generates the strategy that underlies sales techniques, business communication, and business and product development.

*Sales* includes convincing a customer to buy a product, and completing a sales transaction, in response to a customer request. Completion of a sales transaction involves the passing over of ownership of an object, or the completion of a service product, by the provider, and the acceptance of the product by the customer. Customer payments are usually included in sales functions, although ongoing payments for account customers can also be included with customer service functions.

This brings us to the next function: *customer service.* It is important to provide a positive interaction to the customer before, during, and after a sales transaction, to enhance customer satisfaction and retain the customer for future sales. The quality of customer service plays an important role in an organization's ability to interact effectively with its environment. Indeed, customer service probably sits at the leading edge of an organization's interaction with its environment.[11] This is why so many organizations place such an emphasis on sub-functions of Customer Service, like call centers. The quality of service provided by customer call centers can either enhance or diminish the customer's experiences with the organization, and in some extreme cases, destroy or severely degrade the organization's effectiveness in its environment.

The final function is difficult to name, but it involves *products.* This process involves researching customer needs and preferences for products and product packaging (product with product and/or service). The results of this research are passed to the middle layer, where the product is developed. At the same time, the pricing of products is usually determined by the cost of products from the middle layer together with the results of market research into competitive products and suitable pricing. Product quality requirements to meet customer expectations are also determined or confirmed here. If the quality of the product does not meet customer expectations, then the product will fail, reducing the organization's effectiveness in its environment. Finally, the rules about products and product packaging are determined here. Such rules may describe which items can be packaged together and which cannot, or which type of customer (or market segment) is eligible for a certain product.

Because of how closely all these functions depend on customer relations, we call this level the "customer facing" component, or the "shop" of the organization. It

---

[11] Refer to material on the emerging discipline of Sales Process Engineering. Also refer to relevant standards in this area, such as ISO 9004:2000 on performance improvement and ISO 10001:2007 on customer service conduct.

is this top level which must interact with a significant part of the organization's external environment.

## Product development and build

These functions deal with assembling, manufacturing, or otherwise making the product. These functions also deal with the development of new products, as well as the enhancement of existing products. We'll discuss some of these functions that are common to commercial organizations.

Most generally, *research* is systematic investigation with an open mind for the expansion of knowledge. This directed or applied research points toward a specific goal, focusing on possible new products, or enhancements to existing products. Research itself uses input from various sources, including an organization's own market research of customer needs and preferences. The aim is to produce a new (or better) product which the organization's competitors cannot match, and which the organization hopes will provide it with enhanced performance in its environment.

*Development* is the process of engineering the product that is the output of research process, into a finished and marketable product. Many group the development process together with research, but the functions are distinct. In most cases, the output from a research initiative is used as the input for a new development project. If a finished, marketable, and manufacture-able[12] product cannot be output from development, then the whole problem must be returned to research for more work on all or just the problem aspects.

Finally, *production* is the function that actually makes or builds the product. For service products, it means completing the physical work which delivers the service. The production function has been the subject of more investigations,

---

[12] In the sense of "produce-able," it can be made, or, for services, the work can be done.

modeling, and refinements, than virtually any other organizational function. As a result, it is probably the most refined, efficient (both economically and ergonomically), and effective process within most organizations. A lot of EA and business process modeling concentrates on this function.

This level is often called the "factory" or "engine room" for the organization. True as this may be, its existence and prosperity depend on the organization's effectiveness within its environment. This level is possibly the most sensitive to changes in that organizational effectiveness (e.g., changes in products, demand for products, and more). We will discuss environmental changes in more detail later.

## Supplies and suppliers

These functions deal with obtaining the supplies or inputs necessary to develop, build, manufacture, or otherwise run the organization. This level is a mirror image of the Customers and Products level, with the organization being in the role of a customer, and the supplies being the products obtained from other organizations or entities. These functions do **not** deal with customer payments for products, but they do deal with payments to suppliers.

The first function is *shopping,* which involves researching or finding supplies and suppliers. This is the process of locating and examining available products (including service products) to suit a stated need and recommending those products which best meet the organization's input requirements. Shopping is a form of market research, but it considers the input side of a business (while most market research focuses on outputs). Shopping for an organization can include the development and publishing of requests for quotations (RFQ) where the requirement is well known, or requests for proposals (RFP) where the requirement is poorly defined.

*Purchasing* is the process of buying the organizations' input requirements. This process includes price and volume negotiations, as well as staging of payments in a way that would be most advantageous for the organization. The chain may end here for intangible items (such as an insurance policy), as you gain ownership of an intangible item immediately after purchasing it. For tangible goods, though, the next two processes are required.

One function is *supply chain management*. This is the process of negotiating and arranging with suppliers and all interconnected organizations involved in the provision of input requirements to bring together all the separate input requirements in the most economically efficient, timely, and advantageous way, for both the organization requiring the input, as well as the supplier network of organizations. Supplier networks and supply chain management have become increasingly important topics due to globalization of large organizations, as well as an increasing focus on such issues as quality, sustainability, and tax efficiencies across different countries' tax regimes. It is also becoming increasingly important for organizations which employ techniques such as "Just In Time" (JIT) to obtain their supplies on a timely basis without the requirement to hold large stocks in reserve.

The next set of functions includes *delivery, storage, and distribution management*. These processes ensure that the input requirements are readily available where and when they are needed. Concepts involved include JIT delivery and minimal stock holdings, just enough to meet immediate needs, plus a small margin for unforeseen circumstances. These processes focus on increasing returns on investment by making the most economically efficient usage of inventory (minimum inventory to meet requirements), on the theory that parts sitting on a shelf are a waste of money and other resources such as building space. These processes are also involved in concepts such as tailored manufacturing where the "standard" product is modified during its build to fit specific customer requirements, or agile manufacturing, where the quantity of product output can be scaled up or down rapidly, in response to changes in their demand.

This level is often called the "warehouse" or "mine," given its connotations of obtaining and storing raw materials in readiness for them being input to the manufacturing stage to be turned into finished products.

# Business management

The management layer is orthogonal to the three horizontal layers discussed above, as this layer is pervasive throughout the organization. Those familiar with foundational concepts in physical dimension will recognize similarities; the three horizontal layers representing the length, breadth, and height dimensions are each affected by the orthogonal dimension of time.

## Management

The term *management* is difficult to define. We all think we know what it means but can't actually get the words out. Those that have tried to define it, often have their definitions criticized for being too broad, too narrow, or missing the point. For the purposes of this book, we will go with the following working definition: "management is the function of coordinating people, processes (activities), and resources towards a predefined goal." As an analogy, the captain of a ship is the manager, guiding the ship to a particular destination (goal), managing the people (his/her crew) in their various activities, and using the available resources at his/her disposal (the ship, its machinery, sensors, and communication and navigation equipment), to achieve that goal. The captain is assisted by the deck and engineering officers, who have specific line management functions themselves. These functions are focused on specific aspects of the ship and its voyage (e.g., navigation, engines, or cargo); the officers manage a sub-group of the total crew. However, the captain has no specific assigned duties other than as overall manager of the ship, and is responsible for everything.

Management in organizations usually consists of five basic functions:

- **Planning**. Working out what needs to be done and how to do it

- **Organizing**. Arranging and coordinating people and resources to carry out the processes and activities identified in the plans

- **Staffing**. Hiring people into jobs identified as needed to carry out the processes and activities for the plan

- **Leading**. Directing, or motivating – guiding people to carry out the processes and activities

- **Monitoring**. Checking the progress of processes and activities against the desired goals

Usually, management in most organizations is structured hierarchically, although there are some organizations using a networked management structure. In the hierarchical model, each level of management, from top down, is responsible for an increasingly narrow and more specialized focus. However, all levels of management carry out the same five basic functions.

The Business management layer also encompasses those functions which are required to support the rest of the organization. These functions, generally categorized as *administration*, include:

- **Payroll**. The process of remunerating the organization's employees

- **Recruitment**. The process of hiring (and parting with) the organization's employees

- **Finance**. The process of tracking the organization's financial performance, and accounting for the movement of monetary resources

- **Information Technology**. The process of planning, developing, providing, and maintaining information systems, technology, and communications systems throughout the organization

- **Assets**. The process of maintaining existing organizational infrastructure resources

- **General Administration**. The miscellaneous processes required to enable the organization to function effectively

## Monitoring and reporting

For the purposes of EA development, we will focus on monitoring. This function is the key to the success of the other four management functions, and is one where information and information technology (IT) can play a key part. The administration functions (in particular, the financial functions) were among the first to be supported with IT in commercial organizations.

In line with management focus and different levels in the hierarchy comes the focus on what is monitored and what feedback (information) is required. The higher the management level, the broader the focus is both internally and externally – the lower the management level, the more tightly focused it becomes. What is monitored also depends on where the management is located. If it's operational management (that is, located in the three layers, or operational in the administration function of the management layer), monitoring is usually internal for the middle layer, and both internal and external for the top and bottom layers.

Monitoring is the function of gathering and examining information on the areas being monitored. Depending on what is being monitored, you may gather data externally or internally, format it into information, and examine it with managers to determine whether further actions are required. These further actions are appropriately called *reactions*, as the organization uses them to adjust its internal processes or external behavior, forming the final part of the feedback loop.

Returning to our earlier analogy, the cat's brain monitors both internal processes (such as digestion and placement of the feet) and external environmental factors (such as the smell of tuna or the sound of a mouse). Monitoring its environment will inform the cat of any dangers (like a snake), competitors (such as another cat), or the presence of its "input" (in this case, potential food, like a mouse). Monitoring its internal processes will inform the cat of any problems, like indigestion from the last mouse it ate, or hunger for its next meal.

Monitoring, therefore, provides the organization with its window on the world and the environment it operates in. Depending on what you monitor, it can also provide a mirror on the organization itself, to see it as others see it. This is the "outside-in" view of the organization. This outside-in view has become more important in recent times as market research leads, with analysis methods such as Porter's Five Forces framework and the PESTEL (Political, Economic, Social, Technological, Environmental, Legal) analysis, to reconnoiter the environment[13] that an organization proposes to operate in. Although originally applied to market research techniques, later in this book we shall use some of the PESTEL analysis topics to apply to EA.

---

[13] Note that in this book, the term "environment" encompasses **all** of the PESTEL components, whereas PESTEL breaks this down into individual parts for analysis, and the second "E" in PESTEL refers specifically to the natural environment (e.g., pollution, ecological factors, weather, and climate).

Monitoring of internal processes and conditions allows an organization to control those processes and adjust internal conditions. Monitoring of external factors allows the organization to adjust its behavior[14] within its chosen environment, with the aim of becoming more successful within that environment. However, monitoring by itself cannot adjust behavior or process. That requires the next step.

## Reactions

In the management cycle of "plan to do it," "get what you need to do it," "do it," and "check what happened," the "check what happened" is the monitoring step we have just discussed. Monitoring provides the feedback. To close the loop, an organization may need to react (do something) in response to that feedback, particularly if the outcomes of its environmental behavior are not what it expected or desired. The process typically proceeds as follows:

- Assess the monitored data
- Interpret the data
- Define any risks to the organization presented by the data
- Identify possible solutions and remedial action (if required)
- Identify risks, costs, and benefits of the solution(s) and remedial action
- Choose best solution and remedial action
- Undertake chosen remedial action and implement the chosen solution(s)
- Monitor for results

At this point the process begins again. However, depending on what happened, the environment in which the organization operates may have changed. In that case, you may also need to change what you are monitoring. The following are two examples of when this might be the case.

---

[14] The outside-in view and the behavior of organizations with respect to their chosen environments, has become a more focused topic with the growth of electronic means of product delivery and customer interactions, brought about by the Internet and the Web.

An audit of a company by government taxation authorities reveals that the company has been incorrectly calculating a particular tax for the past 5 years. This leads to a notice to pay back taxes, and a lot of unfavorable publicity in the local press. Internal checks reveal that a tax-calculation algorithm in a computer system has been incorrectly set up, and inadequately tested. To counter the bad publicity, the organization pays for an advertisement in the same local press, explaining what happened, and why, and the corrective actions it has undertaken. At this point the organization would again monitor the outcomes of its advertising campaign and decide whether further action should be taken.

Another example involves an appliance store that has identified a set of potential customers for its wares. However, market research has shown that these potential customers are unaware of the shop's existence. A budget is drawn up for a marketing campaign targeting just these potential customers. It includes extensive media advertisements, as well as targeted letterbox drops of advertising material. Before the campaign starts, the success criteria for the campaign is defined as being new sales made to customers in the category targeted. To do this, the shop's sales system is modified to enable point of sale employees to collect certain customer data. This data is now monitored to ascertain whether the investment in the marketing campaign has been successful, as defined by the success criteria.

## Reconfiguration

Under certain circumstances, organizations may need to re-organize, re-structure and re-configure themselves to operate more effectively in their chosen environment. This may be the result of adverse outcomes of its behavior in the environment picked up through monitoring, a combining with another organization through takeovers or mergers, a splitting of the organization into sub-organizations, or disposal of parts of the organization to other organizations or outsourcing of some functions.

However, organizations often undertake re-organization, re-structuring, or reconfiguration because of perceived or actual under-performance, or because of perceived advantages to be gained by so doing. We will use the term "reconfiguration" to include all these changes in organizational structure and basic processes.

Any organizational reconfiguration will impact an existing EA. The most obvious impact is on the internal-facing section of the EA, and traditionally, enterprise architects have tended in the past to concentrate on these aspects. However, the external-facing portion of the EA may also be impacted, but in more subtle ways, as the organization's behavior changes towards its environment. This depends very much on the reconfiguration that is undertaken.

In cases of reconfiguration, where two or more organizations combine such as through a takeover, enterprise architects have tended to look only at how to combine the two sets of IT. Although necessary to consider that, this book is suggesting that looking internally first to see how to combine/integrate existing IT from the two or more organizations, is getting the cart before the horse. What enterprise architects should first look at is how the environment for the combined organizations now looks (i.e. what has changed). Of particular significance are the products, customers, suppliers, and business arrangements. Taken together, these components give an idea of what the company will really need going forward in this new external operational environment.

If the environment has changed, then the next major question to ask concerns the integration of these changes. How do the existing IT environments inherited into the combined organization successfully service the new organization in its new environment? Given that any reconfiguration of this nature would probably now see the organization operating in a significantly changed environment, taking this approach could save a lot of time and effort and therefore money.

Note that a simple change in ownership doesn't typically constitute a full reconfiguration. Examples like these are found when the majority shareholder changes, the umbrella organization (or "holding company") spins off the organization to another owner, but the organization's external environment (e.g., products and customers) do not change. Changes to these factors may be introduced later by the new owner, but the simple change of ownership, by itself, is not really a true reconfiguration.

In summary, organizational reconfigurations may lead to quite complex scenarios for enterprise architects to handle. As a result, this book cannot be prescriptive about what to do to tackle the problem of changing the EA for the reconfigured organization. However, two guiding principles may be of assistance:

- Examine the re-configured organization's external environment, especially in the areas of products, customers, suppliers, and business arrangements. If that has changed, then this will affect the internal ICT.

- Note the changes to the environment and consider the internal ICT, especially with the question of "does it now support the organization for its new environment?"

## Monopoly organizations

A monopoly organization is one which has enough control over a product to significantly determine the terms on which other entities have access to it. A monopoly organization is the only practical provider of the product (including services) in the environment it operates in. Monopolies are characterized by a lack of competition, and a lack of suitable substitutes for its products. A monopsony organization, in contrast, is the only buyer (or customer) for a product within a particular environment.

Monopoly organizations can form naturally, or through mergers, or simply are monopoly organizations because of what they provide, such as government organizations, including national defense forces, or regulatory authorities, or government granted private/semi-private monopoly organizations. For commercial organizations, economic competition usually exists somewhere, if the market is broad enough, especially if free trade and the internet are included as channels of distribution, but there may be monopoly situations forming if the market or distribution channels are narrowed, such as if the only supermarket is in a town where the nearest competition is too far away for customers to feasibly travel to. This is simply a thumbnail sketch of monopoly organizations, and there is ample literature available on the subject, which we won't try to cover here.

What is interesting to the development of an EA, however, is the behavior and structure of monopoly organizations, including:

- Lowered sensitivity to environmental changes, which may take the form of lower or less effective environmental monitoring

- Slower response times to changes in its environment

- Internal processes which are not optimized for efficiency

- Reliance on "inside-out" structures and practices, which force the customer to conform to the organization's way of doing business (rather than the way the customer would prefer to do business)[15]

---

[15] In marketing terminology, the opposite of "enhanced customer experience."

However, just because an organization is a monopoly within its environment, does not mean that it is immune to environmental changes and pressures. It still needs to operate within that environment, and the EA developed for it still needs to take that environment (particularly customers, products, and business arrangements) into account.

---

## Complex organizations

At the beginning of this chapter we said that the three-plus-one model fitted *almost* all organizations. However, there are some, usually very large organizations, where just a single simple three-plus-one model cannot fully describe them. These complex organizations have arranged themselves into a series of "silos", commonly along product lines. Usually each silo produces one or more related types of products, and there can be a number of silos, each with different sets of products. All silos however are responsible to one overarching Business Management function. Figure 6 illustrates such a structure.

Figure 6: The "three-plus-one" layered structure as silos in a complex organization.

| Overall or Group Business Management | | |
|---|---|---|
| **Business Management** | **Business Management** | **Business Management** |
| Customers & Product Sales | Customers & Product Sales | Customers & Product Sales |
| Product Development & Product Build | Product Development & Product Build | Product Development & Product Build |
| Suppliers & Supplies | Suppliers & Supplies | Suppliers & Supplies |
| Silo 1 | Silo 2 | Silo 3 |

Figure 6 also shows each silo with its own Business Management layer, all reporting to the overall or Group Business Management. There are many variations on this structure, including:

- Each silo and the Group Business Management can have its own administrative support units (including accounts, personnel, and IT functions), essentially functioning as an independent business (supported by the Group Business Management's administrative functions)

- Administrative support units could be provided by the Group Business Management, as shared functions between all the silos

- Individual silos (which are largely independent with their own administrative functions) can be listed separately on stock exchanges, while the majority holding or ownership remains with the Group Business Management

Readers could probably find more variations, as well as examples of organizations which have arranged themselves in this manner.

Despite the many variations, the fact remains that the basic organization model of three-plus-one remains as the foundation model, and we will continue to use this model throughout the rest of this book. Thus readers can think of complex organizations as multiples of, or variations on the simpler three-plus-one model.

# CHAPTER 4

# A New Enterprise Architecture

In this chapter we will discuss how to develop the new enterprise architecture (EA). The new EA will:

- Build on the internal view of the organization, provided by existing EA frameworks, and add the external environmental view.

- Provide links from objects in the organization's environment to objects in the internal view. These links will provide the mechanisms for identifying and driving change in the internal EA, based on real changes in the environment.

- Identify possible change vectors for external environment objects. This will provide us with a structured approach to predicting change.

By combining the above three major areas into our existing EA, we will be better placed to develop a future target architecture, which may in fact cater for expected changes. The reason for this is that we will provide:

- A method to link internal and external objects within the EA

- A structured method for examining environmental objects for possible change

- A more objective prediction of change

# Change

Future change is of some concern to managers when they consider proposed investment, especially investment in expensive infrastructure like IT. Although proposed investment in IT may be to correct current problems, most proposed investment will have to take future change into consideration. However, unless we are very structured about how we proceed in evaluating possible change, we will be doing little more than guessing and crystal-ball gazing.

Like all large problems, we will begin by breaking it down into smaller problems and trying to solve each one, within an overall framework. The approach we will use is to consider each external environmental object or factor separately, then link that to internal objects, after which we will try to determine how the environmental object or factor may change. The change vector is what the change may be and the direction of change.

By approaching the problem of change in this way, we may even go further to determine change vectors by applying probability and other statistical methods. This is like the approach used in climate science to predict climate change. It is common for some organizations to use, for example, Monte Carlo methods for predicting probabilities of change in selected parts of their environment. Monte Carlo methods are useful for modeling phenomena with significant uncertainty in inputs, such as the calculation of risk and change.

Whether or not we use statistical methods to predict change, what we gain by this approach is a better understanding of the environment and how this may change, and what the change signifies in terms of the internals of the organization, including its EA.

# Standard model

Up to this point, we have discussed several concepts and ideas. Now we need to start to tie these to an important standard architectural model. In this book, apart from some exceptions, whenever we discuss data, we have generally stayed at the "subject area" level – that level which groups like data entities together. Before proceeding any further, though, we need to specify what those subject areas are, and how they relate to each other. Figure 7 illustrates the data subject areas for every organization.

Figure 7: Standard data subject area model for organizations.

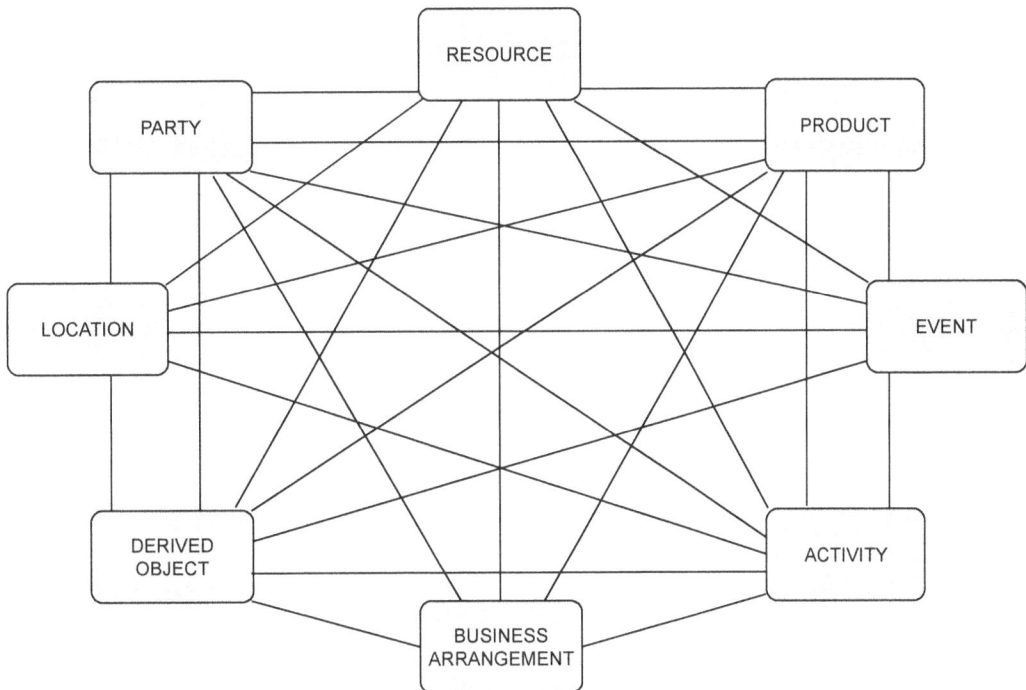

This is a standard model of every organization's data subject areas. The underlying detailed models of data within each of these subject areas may vary from organization to organization, but the subject areas enveloping them will remain the same.

# Party

In this and the following sections we will be discussing the concept of the Party, such as customer, supplier, or employee. To an experienced enterprise architect practitioner, the concept of a party is well known and understood, but that may not be the case for others reading this book, hence this explanation. Briefly, the idea of a generic party comes about because the same person or organization can play many roles with respect to the organization, such as customer, supplier, and employee.

The problem comes if one tries to implement, say a customer database, where the same person can appear as a customer, while also being an employee. If there was also an employee database, that person would be duplicated in both the customer and employee databases, and duplication of data is to be avoided. Duplication also exists in the case of organizations, for example an organization that is both a supplier and a customer.

This gave rise to the Party concept in modeling, whereby a Party can be one of the following:

- A person

- An organization (or a formalized sub-organization within a larger agency, though usually we refer to top-level organizations)

- A work group, such as a project team, that functions as an organization for a limited period of time

From that the Party then plays a role, or multiple roles, with other things. These roles can be played both at any one time, or over time. Having done that, the Party can be developed and implemented as a single non-duplicated database of persons and organizations, each playing roles. The Party database would then be shared between different business application systems. This is the "ideal" solution to the duplication problem.

The trouble is that we do not live in an ideal world. Popular COTS products usually do not come with Party databases, which could be shared with virtually every other business application system requiring access to one or another Party in a role.

We therefore acknowledge that reality in this book, and assume there will be separate customer, employee, and supplier systems and databases. This will inevitably lead to duplication of party information across the organization, and, unsynchronized party information over time (different addresses for a Party, only one of which is the actual correct address). This may become a serious problem in the organization, or it may be a problem that the organization has learned to live with. Coping mechanisms can be designed and implemented, but that is not the focus of this book.

## Environmental entities

There are certain environmental entities that are especially important in containing the factors of change.

### Products

As already discussed, an organization's products are the reason the organization exists. In marketing terms, the product exists to meet a need or demand fulfilled by the product. It is this need or demand which is "supplied" or defined by customers for the product. We see this especially when a new product is brought to market – it either supplies an existing identified and so-far unfulfilled need/demand, or it creates a new need/demand. For commercial organizations, the success of their products (commonly defined by a number of factors, such as product profitability and number of units sold), is also governed by attributes such as price, availability, channel distribution, quality, and similar attributes for competitors' products.

Shifting demand (including decreasing demand to the point of no demand) for an organization's product(s) may be the most common environmental change that the organization experiences. Organizations react to this shift in demand in different ways, depending on the direction of the change.

In my experience, EA practitioners rarely even model products, and, where they do, usually only tag them with the minimal attributes or associated objects of price or channel distribution. Yet demand for an organization's products is very important at the least, if not a determining factor in the organization's behavior within its environment.

In our new EA therefore, we will pay close attention to an organization's products. Not only do we need to model the standard stuff about products like price, but we also need to cater to *demand* for the product. The demand concept also leads us to the next subject, customers, who generate that demand.

However, to account for demand (in an EA sense), first we need to be able to define what a product is, then define some attributes for products.

A Product (an object or service or such intangibles as information) is what an organization makes or assembles from inputs it receives from suppliers, and to which the organization adds value through the use of its own resources and the activities of its personnel. A Product is supplied to the organization's Customer(s) either as a single item or service, or, more commonly, as a package of things, which often include services such as installation services, even if the product is a service product.

We also need to be able to identify what some attributes for the concept of demand may be. To do this, we should look at the study of Economics, which treats demand in a sophisticated and mathematical way. In Economics, demand (i.e. the quantity of a product that can be sold) is a factor of:

- Its price, as an attribute of the product

- The willingness and/or ability of the customer to buy (which in turn is governed by many factors including income and desire for the product)

- The time period, which is the number of products sold in a particular day, month, or year

- The nature of any relevant relationships (e.g., price and quantity demanded have an inverse relationship, which is an attribute of demand)

Other factors include:

- Price of related goods

- Preferences of potential customers

- Potential customers' expectations about future price movements and future income

Demand in Economics is a field unto itself, and not the subject of this book. Demand generation is also a separate area of study in marketing, also not the subject of this book. However, demand for a product is an environmental factor which does impact an organization, and thus its EA. Demand for the organization's products is thus derived from attributes of Customer, Product, and the Customer Order event.

Another important aspect of demand involves the *probability* attribute of the *Customer Order* event entity. Demand could be expressed as an increase in the *probability* value of the Customer Order event occurring. We could link various organizational activities, such as marketing and advertising, with changes in the value of the *probability* attribute of the **Customer Order** event type. The value of the *probability* attribute could also be linked to other attributes, such as the *price* attribute of the Product type. If we increased the value in the *price* attribute of the Product type, according to the inverse relationship rule, we would decrease the value in the *probability* attribute of the Customer Order event type. This may seem obvious to business people outside of the IT/EA world, but these kinds of linkages (let alone modeling the entities and attributes) are not typically considered in traditional EAs.

Before we list the common attributes of Products, we need to separate the *type* of product (which is listed in the product catalog) from the *instance* of product (which is the one individual product I bought and now own, use, or have access to use, e.g. insurance policies or bank credit lines). Common attributes of Product *type* include:

- **Identification of type**. This includes (if the product is a thing) the name of the make, the name or number of the model, and the product description.

- **Price of type**. There can be multiple pricings available on a product, such as cost price, list price, floor price, price for the purchase of one versus multiple items, and maybe a special sale price. This is why data modelers usually treat "price" as a separate entity in their data model – a process known as *normalization*.

- **Product packaging**. Often products comprise several sub-products (other complete products that could be sold individually), and also product features (attributes that cannot be sold individually, such as color).

Note that not all of the component sub-products and/or product features are made or supplied by the organization. The car's alternator is rarely made by the organization which makes the car. Products consisting of other products or features are product packages.

It is extremely important to understand the difference between a component sub-product and a product feature. The sub-product can be sold separately -- for example, as a spare part later in the life of the product, or offered "a la carte." However, the product feature cannot "stand on its own," and makes no sense to be sold separately; for example, you can't *just* buy the color of something. However, that does not prevent sub-products and product features in a package from being priced separately. This means that even though you couldn't buy a "limited-edition color scheme" by itself (without also buying the car, phone, or whatever it is), the company can still charge you extra for that special paint job.

Common attributes of Product *instance* include:

- **Identification**. Some of these (if the product is a thing), such as name, make, model, model number, and product description are inherited from product *types*. Others, such as serial number, are not inherited, and are often used to identify the particular instance of the product. In the case of service products, the date and time that the service was provided are good identifiers.

- **Price at which the instance was sold**. Note that this may have been a negotiated price, different from the list price. In a good product/sales application, the individual prices of the component products or product features should also be recorded.

- **Date and time of sale**, which are often important for warranty sub-products or Business Arrangements.

Note that there are some types of products which are sometimes difficult to comprehend. One example is shares in an organization. Shares provide investors with both beneficial ownership in an organization (by paying out dividends based on profit earned to shareholders), *and* can be traded for a profit or loss just like any other commodity. Organizations exist whose only product is to make money for their shareholders, by buying and selling shares for a profit. Other financial instruments beyond shares may also be traded for a profit, but those are beyond the scope of this book.

## Customers

Customers (actual, potential, or possible) consume products, and create the demand for those products. Customers for an organization's products may be identified by name (or by other details), or anonymous. Typically, "cash-and-carry" customers are anonymous customers. Customers may be individuals or organizations.

A Customer is a Party (a person or organization) that interacts with the organization through its Products. This includes both the parties that purchased or paid for the product as well as the end user of the product, and any other party which has an interest[16] in the product. It excludes any party which supplies a component of the product (or product package), like a financial component of the package such as a loan to purchase the product.

Customers are obviously of primary importance to any organization, as an organization would cease to exist without them. Customers must therefore be modeled as part of the new EA.

---

[16] For example, an application for a patent or trademark, a product of the government patents office, where several parties may be associated with the product – those who apply for the patent/trademark, those who are advocates for the applicant(s), those who are associated with the applicant(s), and those who oppose the application and their associates and their advocates.

Common attributes of Customer usually include:

- **Identification**. These are attributes that separate customers into individuals (or organizations). If the customer is an organization, we usually want to know the identity of some contact person within that organization. If an organization's customers are anonymous, identification usually becomes generic, and grouped into areas covered by demographics.

- **Location**. These are attributes concerned with addresses, such as physical locations of customers. These attributes are often important in determining such things as distribution channels to be used for products, and other location-dependent issues.

- **Demographics**. These attributes (sometimes including location) provide more data about customers, and include, where applicable, age, gender, education levels, employment status and employment type (e.g. permanent or part-time). Demographic attributes often allow an organization to better understand its customers.

- **Ability to purchase**. Discussed above in connection with demand, this is basically the customer's available income to spend on the product. This attribute does not usually apply to products provided free of charge.

- **Propensity to purchase**. Also discussed above in connection with demand, this is the customer's requirement or desire for the product. This attribute does apply regardless of whether there is a charge for the product.

In my experience, most organizational EAs trying to model customers will stop after identification and location, ignoring the last three attribute groups. Yet it could be argued that these last three attributes (and changes to them) most directly impact an organization.

## Suppliers and items supplied

Organizations are also customers of other organizations' and people's products including services (excluding, for this discussion, services provided to the organization by its own employees.) These products are used as inputs to the organization's own product manufacturing process. Without the products provided by its suppliers, organizations would have no products of its own. Consequently, these need to be also included in the new EA.

Common attributes of a supplier include:

- **Identification**. Broadly as above for customers, although it is unusual for there to be anonymous suppliers

- **Location**. Broadly as above for customers. Location dependent issues, in the case of suppliers, tend to impact on logistics and supply-chain considerations. Note that if logistics, in the way of transport, are provided by other organizations, then these must be added as suppliers of input products.

- **Capacity to supply**. These attributes include financial viability, dependency on this organization (is this organization their only or main customer?), and the legal status of the supplier (for example, is it incorporated?). Of increasing relevance in globalized economies are such things as the suppliers' treatment of their workforce, business ethics, and other related social issues.

Items supplied or supplies including services, are those things that the organization uses as input to its product production. Common attributes of items supplied include:

- **Prices of supplied items**, considering monetary rates of exchange where applicable. Prices may also include costs of logistics (including storage costs and related storage issues)

- **Maximum quantities** able to be supplied

- **Lead times for re-order** (which includes lead times due to logistics requirements)

Alternative or equivalent supply items, including all the above, plus suppliers of the alternatives, should also be included into the EA modeling. Even though the shipping logistics are included as part of the supplied item, logistics services should be treated as any other input supply item: a product with a supplier and a supply item (the delivery service). The reason for this is contained in the importance attached to supply chain management[17] in many organizations, and the impacts on its own product production due to logistic disruptions.

Financial supplies (such as loans and overdrafts) and their suppliers (such as financial institutions) should also be considered, as many organizations depend on these to remain viable. Finance can be for capital expenditure such as a loan for a new type of machine, or for operational expenditure such as overdraft facilities and export-import financial instruments. Suppliers of finance can be traditional banks or other organizations. As financial supplies can have fixed or variable costs, they need to be considered for an EA, as they may generate change.

## Business arrangements

As discussed earlier, the business arrangement concept covers a number of areas which govern the organization's behavior. Because each of these concepts is so closely tied to the EA, a change to any of these factors (for example, the passage

---

[17] Note that "supply chain management" considers the movement from supplier, through the three tiers of the organization to its customer. Supposing we were developing an EA for Org A, and Org B was a supplier to Org A. From the point of view of this book and Org A's EA, Org A is the end-user customer for Org B. Whilst supply chain management could include Org B's own supply chain to Org A, for the purposes of Org A's EA we will ignore Org B's supply chain, to avoid being recursive.

of a new law or a change in a contract) will in turn create major changes for the EA.

- **Legal**. Any laws with which the organization must comply, and which govern its internal and external behavior. This includes legal frameworks in every country in which the organization operates (including through its distribution channels).

- **Agreements**. These can be formal (such as a contract) or informal (such as a verbal commitment). Informal agreements are not necessarily as relaxed as the name implies; in some cases, they can be as binding as formal agreements.

- **Customer accounts**. These are basically agreements between the organization and its customers to use or purchase the organization's products and pay later (or incrementally at set intervals).

- **Standards**. These have been developed to establish a norm or requirement and can relate to several areas including objects (technical standards) or services (behavioral standards) or processes (what must be done). The main purpose of standards is to establish a minimum or baseline quality of the delivered product, and addresses such areas as safety, usability, and inter-operability.

- **Commonly accepted practices**. These include voluntary codes of conduct and overt behavior, as well as implied behavior (such as "fit for purpose"). Commonly accepted practices may vary with location but are mainly governed by expectations between parties. Commonly accepted practices should not conflict with applicable laws.

- **Shares and related financial interests in the organization**. The purchase of shares creates a business arrangement between the organization and the investor. Both parties have expectations of each other – most notably the investor's expectation to be paid dividends at regular intervals.

Common attributes of Business Arrangement include:

- **Identification**. Lists of parties (people and organizations) who agreed to the business arrangement, and parties affected by the arrangement

- **Location**. Places where the parties are located, and places where the business arrangement applies

- **Subject matter**. The business arrangement should always pertain to something else found in the organization's EA

- **Time**. The start (and possibly the finish) dates when the business arrangement applies.

For the new EA, research should be done to establish the links between business arrangements and whatever else they cover in their subject matter in the EA.

## Events

Events are the main environmental occurrences to which organizations must respond. An Event is something that happens; and can be grouped into broad classes. Events are modeled as Event Types (descriptions of potential events that could happen), and Event Instances (individual events that have actually happened). The following are some examples:

- **Customer events**. These include such things as orders for products, payments made, complaints, contacts with organization officers, and changes to the customer's circumstances such as a change of address which affect the organization in some way.

- **Supplier events**. These include such things as issuing invoices or other notices to the organization, and events impacting the supply chain for input products to the organization.

- **Product events**. These are unexpected things that happen to the organization's products. One example is a previously undiscovered defect in a product, such as a phone battery catching fire under normal usage conditions. These may also include events associated with *known* product defects, but which were not disclosed or fixed.

- **Resource events**. These are events which occur to the resources used by the organization to conduct its business. Examples may include water damage to stored goods through a broken water pipe in the organization's warehouse, or a broken machine used in the product manufacturing process.

- **Human events**. These can range from civil unrest to an accident to one or more employees causing disruptions to the organization's operations.

- **Natural events**. These include fire, storm or weather damage, flooding, or any other natural event, which may cause disruptions to the organization's operations.

Events may trigger other events, leading to a chain of events. For example, a natural event such as a lightning strike may lead to a resource event such as the outage of a communications network node.

Typical attributes of Event include:

- **Identification**. This is usually the event name and type.

- **Time**. The date and time of the event occurrence. Many events are point events which occur at a point in time but have little noticeable duration, while other events may have a significant duration.

- **Probability**. This is the chance of the event occurring.[18] Note that the inverse of the probability of an event occurring does not necessarily indicate the probability of the event not occurring. If an event has a 70% probability of occurring, it does not necessarily follow that it also has a 30% probability of not occurring. Note also that the Probability attribute applies only to Event types and not to the Event instance itself.

- **Links**. This connects the event to other entities or objects which are affected by the event, or, as in the case of activities, are triggered by, or trigger the event. This could also include links to locations where the event occurs.

Event types do not have the attributes of time and date of the event, as this usually applies only to event instances, unless we knew beforehand that the event would take place.

Events should always link to activities which are the organization's response to the event, or the activities which are designed to either trigger or not trigger the event. Organizations usually have a structured response prepared for most common and obvious events. However, the less common types of events are not usually linked to a structured response, unless organizations have prepared a business continuity plan, or other contingency plans for events such as product failures and recalls. Sadly, most business continuity plans are developed by the IT department, and thus usually only address the continuance of provision of IT services to the organization. Although important (because IT has taken over many business processes), this does not represent the total problem space.

Events should also be linked to the other entities, external and internal, that they impact. These include the resources used by the organization, business

---

[18]  For purposes of this book, we will assume a simple single-number probability value here. However, for those practitioners of statistical mathematics, the probability of an event occurring or not occurring can be a far more complex set of calculations – refer to the literature about AI and subjects such as the Bayes estimator.

arrangements which govern the organization's behavior, its products, and customers. In fact, events may influence or affect virtually every other entity.

# Internal entities

Internal entities are what most traditional EAs focus on including the organizational structure, business process (linked activities), and the resources such as information technology required by the organization. These represent the "anatomy" of the organization, and are still essential in the new EA. It must be stressed that the new EA proposed in this book does not dismiss the areas covered under traditional EAs. Instead it builds on these to provide a richer more complete view of the organization.

## Organizational structure

Organizational structures are grouped around task allocation, supervision, and coordination activities, all of which are aimed at achieving the organization's goals, such as the provision of products to its customers. Most, although not all organizations are hierarchical in structure, although a distinction must be made between formal and informal organizational structures. Organizational structures are usually developed to enhance efficiencies in deploying repeatable processes, their supervision and coordination, while confining decision-making to a select few whose views shape the organization and its behavior within its environment.

This book is not about organizations and their structures. Instead EA simply describes organization structures as it finds them. However, organization structures do change, sometimes in response to external environmental events, or sometimes due to perceptions of managers that a different structure will provide better performance in some way. EA practitioners should be at least aware of different general types of structures and the reasons for them. Organizational structures are modeled as subtypes of the Party entity.

Organizational structures are usually divided into 3 basic sub-classes, namely:

- **Permanent (or formal) organizational structures** include divisions and functional groupings. These can usually be modeled as hierarchies, or inter-connected hierarchies. The term "permanent" is used in a relative sense, as these are usually longer-lasting than the "temporary" structures described below. Permanent organizational structures are often known by the generic term "organization units".

- **Formal "people responsibility" chains** are "A reports to B" type diagrams, and are usually hierarchical or matrix-like.

- **Temporary organizational structures**. These structures are assembled to achieve a limited, short-term objective (i.e. a project), and are often called work groups. Some work groups are not temporary (a standing committee), in which case they are a part of the permanent organizational structure.

Typical attributes for organizational structures include:

- **Identification**. The name of the organization unit, position, or person

- **Location**. Where the organization unit/person is physically located, as well as contact details for the unit/person

- **Function**. Usually the formal function of the unit, or functional title of the person

- **Links**. These are the links to other units or persons, which describe hierarchies or matrices or chains.

Organization units or people are also often linked to activities and resources.

## Activities

An Activity is something which people or computer systems do. A linked set of activities, or activity chain, constitutes a process. Activities can be decomposed into lower level activities. "Run project" can be decomposed into the individual project activities. This decomposition of activities is sometimes called a "work breakdown structure" (WBS). Theoretically there is no limit to the levels of decomposition of activities. Practically, one would not go lower than what makes sense within a given context. There is no point to describing an activity at any level of finer detail than the context requires.

There are three basic types of activities:

- **The "doing" activity**. This is simply represented by "do something," such as "Run Project".

- **The "decision" activity**. This is represented as a question, usually with a binary ("yes" or "no") answer, and leads to branching of the activity chain. Business process modeling practitioners prefer to use decision activities with only binary answers.[19] As such, complex decisions (which may result in more than two answers) are usually broken down into a series simpler of linked decisions with binary answers. This series of linked decisions is called a "decision tree."

- **A milestone**, which typically has no duration, or assigned people or resources. Milestones usually only have limited uses, such as in projects,

---

[19]  Computer programming languages usually also provide a second type of decision construct, namely the "case" statement: case x = blue then do A, case x = green then do B, case x = yellow then do C, else for all other cases do D. This provides a simple way of coding a multiple branch problem, saving time in coding the same problem as a multiple series of binary branches.

to mark completion of a series of linked activities, so we will basically ignore these. However, they may be used to good effect in activities such as installation of a product.

Business rules are usually modeled as decision trees, and the IT world has numerous examples of commercial off-the-shelf (COTS) products which are "business rules engines." The IT world also has numerous examples of COTS products which are "workflow engines," driving the linked series of "doing" activities, some of which may be carried out by a person, and some of which are carried out by a computer program, such as emailing a document to somebody in the organization. There are even examples of COTS products which do both.

Activities can be triggered by other activities or by events. The former illustrates the relationships between activities. The most common of these is the "Finish-Start" relationship, where the completion of one activity triggers the start of the next activity. However, there are other relationships, such as:

- **"Start-Start,"** where two activities run in parallel, and must start at the same time

- **"Finish-Finish,"** where two activities run in parallel, and must finish at the same time

- **"Parent-Child,"** where the start of an activity (the parent) is the trigger for starting the first of its more detailed (the child) activity.

In the final case, the finish of the last child activity also finishes the parent activity. A branch out of the sequence of child activities for parent A, into child activities of parent B signifies the finish of parent A, if there is no return path from the child activities of parent B. Activities can also be triggered by events. In some organizations, types or classes of events are linked to types or classes of activities (a planned process template), so that the actual occurrence of the event results in the implementation of the planned process.

Some activities are undertaken to avoid classes or types of events, such as those activities undertaken to avoid adverse events occurring like securing a cliff face to avoid a landslide. The discipline of risk management attempts to list and categorize adverse classes or types of events, assign some measure of the likelihood of their occurrence and the impact if they did occur, and plan or undertake activities to avoid (or reduce the likelihood of) their occurrence, or, should they occur, respond to their occurrence. At the same time, some activities are undertaken to encourage (or increase the probability of) certain events occurring. Examples of these include advertising and marketing activities to increase the probability of customer order events for the organization's products.

Common attributes of activities include:

- **Identification**. This includes the name and type or class of activity.

- **Duration time**. This represents the actual duration when the activity took place. In organizations with pre-planned process templates (activity types/classes), it is common to include expected duration, or even more sophisticated minimum, maximum, and expected durations. Adding these together using the relationships between activities provides estimates of how long the chain of activities (the process) is likely to take, thus forming an estimate of effort and duration.

- **Effort time**. This measures the work required to complete the activity. If an activity is estimated at 8 hours of effort, this would take one person one day duration (assuming a standard 8-hour working day) to complete the activity, or two persons half a day duration (4 hours effort each, assuming 100% allocation to each, and that each person shares equally in the work). In organizations with pre-planned process templates, it is common to include expected effort, or even more sophisticated minimum, maximum, and most likely expected effort.

- **Assignments**. These are people and resources (like machine tools) assigned to an activity.

- **Activity links**. These are the relationships between this activity and other activities.

- **Event links**. These are relationships between the activity and the event(s) which triggered it, or the events which the activity triggers.

- **Other links**. These are relationships with other entities (such as customers) which are involved with, or affected by, the activity.

## Resources

These are things (*not* people) which the organization uses to carry out its activities. While the term "resource" might typically refer to a natural resource (like a source of water or wood), in this book resources are those things required to produce the organization's products and for the organization to operate effectively. This excludes input products used to make the organization's output products. For example, a mining company would use the iron ore in the ground as an input product, their mining machinery as a resource to extract it, and the broken up and transportable iron ore as their output product.

Common resources include buildings, vehicles, machinery, information and communications technologies (ICT), and office equipment. Accountants make a distinction between capital expenditure, which are those resources that the organization purchases outright, and operational expenditure which are those resources that are purchased on a usage basis, such as electricity, telecommunications, and water. Given that some resources, like buildings, vehicles, and machinery, may be leased, and thus come out of operational expenditure, and that other resources like electricity can be argued to be input raw material products, it may be difficult to draw the line between what is a resource, and what is an input raw material product. The terms "infrastructure" and "asset" are good synonyms for resource.

To further clarify this concept, here are some examples of resources, taken from different types of organization:

- **Telecommunications companies**. Their installed network, including exchange equipment

- **Mining companies**. Their mining machinery and developed mining infrastructure they have directly invested in, such as mine structure and specialist equipment

- **Manufacturing companies**. Their equipment used to build things in the factory

- **Financial companies**. The money or cash available to them to provide financial products to their customers, as well as the computers and programs used to manage the money

Attributes for resources vary according to the resource. However, the following are some typical attributes:

- **Identification**. Examples include name, type, or class of item, and serial number, make, model, and registration number.

- **Source**. For example, manufacturer and vendor

- **Location**. For mobile resources (such as vehicles), this may be where it is currently located, or where it is usually located

- **Purpose**. The intended use of the resource

- **Links**. Relationships with other activities, events, business arrangements, and products related to a particular resource

# Links

Identifying links between external objects or entities and internal objects or entities is one of the keys to a new enterprise architecture. The reason is that changes in the organization's environment, represented by the external objects or entities, will demand changes to the organization's internal objects or entities. These changes are transmitted or triggered via links. In this section we will:

- Search for candidate links.

- Demonstrate how the links transmit or trigger change within the organization.

To be of real use, we then need to examine in which direction the change will occur. This is called the change vector.

## Candidate links

Links form between objects/entities when there is a relationship of some kind between them. There are two basic types of relationships: overt and common value.

Overt relationships are relationships which can be identified and named, for example "Person *drives* Car," where Person and Car are two objects or entities, and *drives* is the relationship. Overt relationships usually have a business context and are subject to business rules. For example, "Only one Person can drive only one Car at any one time." As in this simple example, overt relationships between two objects or entities can be expressed as simple sentences. Whether it's active or passive, the verb in the sentence should be the same or equivalent, such as "drives" and "is driven by." Overt relationships on EA models are usually displayed as lines.

Common value relationships are relationships which come about because two objects happen to share the same or linked values in an attribute of each. Most common of these is where a date value is the same for both. For example, two people, not otherwise related, can share the same date of birth.

Common value relationships are often used in the marketing and survey industries. For example, all people who live in a given postal area, as identified by the postcode attribute of their location. Another type of linked value relationship we mentioned earlier, was the inverse relationship between the value of the price attribute of a product and the value of the probability attribute of a customer order event. However, we will continue to refer to both of these types as common value relationships.

## Overt Relationships

In most EA methodologies, overt relationships between objects are implemented as common attributes, one in each object, one or both of which act as a "pointer" to the other object instance. Thus, in our simple example, "Person *drives* Car," the Car object may hold the identity attribute of the Person object, signifying that this Person instance is now driving this Car instance.

The Person identity attribute within the Person object is called the *primary key* of Person and identifies a single example of the Person object. The Person identity attribute within the Car object is called the *foreign key* of Person within the Car object and acts as a pointer from the instance of the Car object to the instance of the Person object driving the car. It is these foreign key attributes we will be looking at for links between external and internal objects.

However, before we do that, there is one other issue we need to look at within overt relationships. Overt relationships have three characteristics, which are:

- **Cardinality**. This is where two objects, linked by an overt relationship, have either a one-to-many, many-to-many, or one-to-one relationship. In the simple example "Person drives Car," this is a one-to-one relationship if, and only if, we ignore the time factor, and talk about "at a single point in time." When we factor in time, we find that we can, over time, have the Person driving many Cars, and the Car being driven by many Persons. We have in fact a many-to-many relationship between Person and Car of the "drive" type. Thus, for the "drives" relationship, we have the additional time dimension attribute.

- **Optionality**. This is where the relationship is defined as "must always" or "may sometimes." If sometimes that Person does not drive that Car (as when the car is parked without a driver), the relationship is optional.

- **Generality**. When we look at all the possible relationships between a Person and a Car, we find that there can be many different types of relationships, such as "owns" and "rents." We can therefore add another attribute to the relationship, "owns" and/or "rents." If we know of exactly one type of relationship between two objects, we can embed that type into the relationship name, carrying that name into the foreign key. However, when multiple types of relationships exist, we can either create more relationships (resulting in more foreign keys – one for each relationship), or we can make a general relationship and attach an attribute which will hold the name.

Out of these three characteristics we can see that overt relationships themselves can have attributes. This is important because a change in the value of an attribute can indicate a change in the environment.

Out of these three characteristics, relationships will always have two (cardinality and optionality). The third characteristic, generality, is a result of how we develop the model for the EA, and how deeply we search for possible changes. If we say that a relationship between two entities will only always be of one type, then we must be sure that the "always" means "always." This is a big call, because using the words "always" and "never" usually leads to being wrong later. If unsure, it is better to model the general relationship and include the "type of relationship" attribute into the normalized structure.

Overt relationships between external entities and internal entities are the main links which transmit change into the organization. We have already discussed or alluded to some of these, for example:

- Event (external) triggering Activity (internal)

- Business Arrangement (external) governing how Activity (internal) is carried out

However, we must also not ignore overt relationships between external entities, for example:

- Event (external) triggered by Customer (external), as in a customer order for a Product

- Clustering of Event types (external) at a Location (external) (for example, lightning strikes on top of a hill, which may be of primary interest to the organization if they wanted to put some equipment Resources on that hill)

One simple example is of the instance of a specific Event type which has an instance of an Activity type mapped to it. If this type of event occurs, we will respond with this type of process. The organization has thus prepared in advance to respond with a process which is activated on the occurrence of that specific event. If a different or new type of event occurs, to which the organization needs to respond, but it has no activity types or process mapped to, or defined for it, then the organization needs to do that. If the systems are already in place for this, then it becomes a matter of the organization simply developing a new process, thus responding rapidly to changes in its environment.

## Common Value Relationships

There are many common value relationships, but only a few of these may be of any significance. For example, a person may be born in Sydney on the same day that a contract was signed between two companies in London. There may be absolutely no significance in the fact that the person has the same date of birth as the contract start date. On the other hand, there are some common value relationships which, depending on the context, do have significance. Common value relationships are frequently found in such things as dates, locations, and monetary values including prices, costs, and incomes. Some examples include:

- Demographic surveys and profiling often use dates of birth, places of birth, and voting patterns for purposes like targeted advertising, or tracking political affiliations. However, for the new EA, demographic data about customers who have common value relationships (e.g., location or income) with an internal entity (e.g., product outlets or prices) should be of significance. In these relationships, a change in the value of one may influence the value of another, and thus impact the EA.

- Event instances have a date and/or time, and often a location, describing when and where they occur. An event such as a lightning strike at a telecoms installation (which is a resource to the telecoms organization) may cause damage to that installation. As such, in this example, the event location and the resource location both share the same values. The lightning strike event would trigger activities by the telecoms organization, like sending out a truck to repair the damage. In a well-run organization, the event type (i.e. lightning striking and damaging a resource) would be already linked to a set of activities defining the response to such an event, should it occur.

We can see from the above examples that common value relationships may indeed impact the organization's EA. In the demographics example, the impact would be if new product outlets, not necessarily physical outlets, may need to be developed. The impact on the EA also lies in the fact that computerized applications need to be developed to track customer demographics and products, including competing products. In the event location example, the impact could be development of workflow (i.e. activities performed sequentially) applications to deal with such events.

Earlier we also mentioned that there was an inverse relationship between the value of a product's attribute, price, and the value of the customer order event's attribute, probability of occurrence. We also call these kinds of relationships common value relationships, as they are based on the values of the attributes. Readers may be able to spot more examples of common value relationships from their own experiences of working with different types of organizations.

## Change transmission

Changes are transmitted via relationships, both overt and common value, and the attributes which implement them. When the value of an attribute occurring in an external entity changes, and that attribute is related to some attribute in an internal entity, it logically follows that the internal entity will change. This may appear like an obvious statement. However, it's this kind of change that we are looking for in the new EA. We need to know what changes in the organization's environment, and what and how that change impacts the organization. Perhaps the best way to explain this is through some examples.

### Scenario 1 – The Car Parts Supplier

Rapid-stop Brakes supplies brake parts for cars built by Superior-Cars. Both Rapid-stop Brakes and Superior-Cars are located geographically close to each other. This makes the logistics costs in getting Rapid-stop Brakes' brake parts to Superior-Cars lower than other possible alternative suppliers, which is a major consideration for Superior-Cars to source these parts from Rapid-stop Brakes. Superior-Cars is also Rapid-stop Brakes' best customer, taking over 80% of

Rapid-stop Brakes' product output – the rest goes mainly to retail chains which stock after-market spare parts.

Rapid-stop Brakes has a supplier contract with Superior-Cars which fixes the price to Superior-Cars, irrespective of logistics costs, for another 5 years, well past the time that Superior-Cars has completed its relocation. A small sales team represents Rapid-stop Brakes directly to its customers, including Superior-Cars. This direct representation is the only method that Rapid-stop Brakes uses to sell its products to customers, as it does not sell directly to the public.

**The change**
Superior-Cars is now going to relocate their manufacturing to another city (the city of Beyondreach) a long way away, to rationalize their manufacturing facilities, while improving access to shipping facilities for export of their vehicles.

In response, Rapid-stop Brakes is proposing to do two things:

- Open a new manufacturing plant to build brake parts for Superior-Cars in Beyondreach. This is deemed more cost effective than taking another 5 years' losses brought about by having to bear the increased logistics costs, as Rapid-stop Brakes would have to do under the current contract.

- Direct sell to the public and to other organizations, via a new website. The aim of this is to broaden the customer base, and perhaps eventually move into international markets.

**EA model indications**
On the EA model the indications of change will include:

- Location of a major customer, Superior-Cars, will change to Beyondreach. This will also be the new delivery address for Rapid-stop Brakes' products to Superior-Cars, presumably with some effective date.

- Rapid-stop Brakes will establish new premises in Beyondreach to manufacture brake parts for Superior-Cars. Rapid-stop Brakes will have a new branch in a different location.

- With the new branch in Beyondreach, Rapid-stop Brakes will either need to source new materials suppliers and/or new logistics suppliers, or change the existing arrangements with current suppliers. In either case, there will be new or changed Business Arrangements with suppliers.

- The new sales channel (represented by the new website) will necessitate changes to logistics (to deliver the product), changes to business arrangements (like product warranties), new or different customers with different locations, as well as impacts of different government taxes and charges (business arrangements again) from a potential international marketplace. New customers and customer locations will also be added.

- International sales through the new website may require new business processes, as well as possible changes to current product pricing structures, as this brings Rapid-stop Brakes into direct competition with other similar parts suppliers. There are also likely to be new event types or classes (both adverse and routine), demanding consideration and new processes to deal with them.

- Resources required by Rapid-stop Brakes will also be impacted, through changes in product manufacturing, distribution, and resource relationships with new activities and events.

**Summary**

These two apparently innocuous changes in the environment will result in major internal changes: a change of location of its primary customer, and the addition of a wider customer base through the new website. These changes will be to both the business in terms of processes, structure, and different events and business arrangements it must deal with, and probably to its ICT infrastructure, both physical and in applications software that need to be deployed. This is one example of how external environmental changes impact on internal enterprise architecture components.

## Scenario 2 – The Government Social Security Department

The Social Security Department's (SSD's) products are a range of government benefits, usually in the form of financial support, although the products can take other forms, such as free or subsidized third-party products/services. SSD's customers (actual or potential) are people whose circumstances mean that they can be included within a set of eligibility criteria, the rules for which are usually set by the government of the day. Thus, eligibility criteria or product rules can be called *features* of any given product. Therefore, the feature set for a product will include all those things (benefits) the product provides, as well as the eligibility criteria (rules) for that product.

When people apply for an SSD product, they can be said to place an order for that product. The customer event of placing the order triggers one or more processes (chains of activities) within SSD. Most of these processes check the customer's detailed circumstances against eligibility criteria, to match the customer with the product which best meets their needs. Once these processes are completed, and the decision made to approve the product for the customer, other processes are triggered to instigate payments for example, to the customer, such as to provide the customer with the product (product provisioning).

In the past, SSD has also been the government's conduit for providing relief payments for people caught in natural disasters, such as flood victims who lose business assets or property. These relief payments may be special products created just for the circumstances (like a special relief fund for a serious hurricane), or standard products (with either standard or modified eligibility criteria) such as payment of unemployment benefits to small business owners who lost business assets.

SSD utilizes a 30-year-old computerized application system to manage all its customers and products. The system uses technology which is no longer sold, and has much embedded code to implement the products, features, and rules/eligibility criteria. Most of the processes associated with product selection and approval for customers are carried out by SSD employees as manual processes. Once products are approved for customers, product delivery and payments are automated (e.g. direct payments into customers' bank accounts), although the product provisioning process is still largely a manual data entry process.

**The change**
A new government is elected with the promise of cutting SSD expenditure, thus reducing the budgetary provision for SSD products, by "tightening-up" the eligibility criteria. After a highly-publicized review, some products are no longer offered, while others have their feature sets, such as benefits and eligibility criteria, changed with the aim of reducing the number of future customers who can be provided with the products, and reducing benefits for existing customers of existing products.

In response, SSD proposes a relatively expensive, one-year project to achieve two goals:

- Modify its computer system to cater for the new/changed products and product features

- Train its employees and modify its manual processes (one example of BPR, Business Process Re-engineering) for the new/changed products and product features

The costs of the project to implement the changes, as proposed by SSD, represent a significant percentage of the government's expected budgetary savings for the changed products.

**EA model indications**

On the EA model, the indications of change will include:

- New or changed Business Arrangements (legislation and related legal instruments). These are framed and passed by the new government to give effect to the changed or deleted Products, and product features (eligibility criteria), and product pricing (benefits).

- Changes to business processes (Activities) in relation to the new, changed, or deleted products. For deleted products, a plan to retire the products must be in place.

- Changes to Product delivery Activities, including automated activities. These are mainly in the automated payment systems, as well as manual processes which surround the product delivery like setting up of payments and monitoring ongoing payments and eligibility.

**Summary**

The kinds of changes described here should be relatively predictable and relatively painlessly implemented in SSD's IT systems, as well as their business processes. However, mainly because of lack of flexibility in SSD's IT systems, these very predictable changes will be difficult, expensive, and take a long time to implement.

**Change vectors**

Knowing that there is going to be a change in something in the environment is useful. It would be even more useful however, to know how, or in which direction, the change will manifest itself. In fact, in most cases, we need to know *both* what will change and how it will change, before we can act on this information. A vector is the direction in which an object is moving; as such, a change vector describes both *what* and *how* it is changing.

In addition to knowing what will change, as well as the way it will change (change vector), it would be extremely useful to know how much will change.

What we really need is to quantify the change vector, although this isn't always possible from a practical standpoint. Some examples may help clarify this idea, so we'll consider two more fictional case studies.

**Example 1**
From years of careful research, ABC Inc. knows that most of its customers come from a very specific socio-economic group and all tend to live in a set of adjoining postal code areas, near ABC Inc.'s outlet store. As some customers have improved their economic means, they have moved out of these areas to neighborhoods of better social status, but have generally been replaced by new customers moving in.

As such, ABC Inc. has had a steady number of customers (albeit individuals have turned over, being replaced by others). However, ABC Inc. also knows that its "previous" customers (those who have now moved away to better areas) would still be customers of ABC if they didn't have to travel so far to do so.

ABC wants to know how many "previous" customers there are in this category, as this could influence whether ABC open another outlet store or invests in an e-store. This is the missing piece of data to completely quantify the change vector. Of course, investing in the online store could in fact provide this missing data. Obviously both these cases, ABC opening a new physical store or a virtual store, would also be of vital interest to the IT department. Thus, establishing one or more new outlets for its products establishes a major change vector for ABC Inc. and its IT department.

**Example 2**
For another example, consider Howes Bus Service – a bus and transport business serving a small regional country town of about 50,000 residents. It provides regular scheduled services along various fixed routes (generally from the suburbs to the town center and return), and including to nearby neighboring towns, school bus services, as well as a limited number of bookable excursion (sometimes called "coach") services.

However, Howes does not run scheduled coach services to other towns and cities. A recent business review revealed that Howes' regularly-scheduled services within the town area were patronized well (and therefore profitable) only in the morning and evening "rush hours," when people generally went to work and returned home. With fewer patrons using the service, daytime hours were generally unprofitable.

A bright young employee suggests Howes starts a new service, whereby town residents can either phone a toll-free number or use the web, to book a "We will pick you up at your door" service. This would involve the customer booking a pickup service and nominating a destination, then being advised as to when approximately the bus would arrive and where its closest pick-up point to the customer's location. Buses would be equipped with a dispatching system in the bus. The bus and driver running the regular route nearest the customer's location, and running to the customer's nominated destination, would be advised by the system, and the bus driver diverted to the customer's location for the pickup, similar to a taxi service. The fare charged would be a little extra on top of the regular fare, but a lot less than a taxi fare, and the service would only be available off-peak.

Naturally, such a change in the normal products provided by Howes would involve a large impact on the IT department. The buses providing this service will need to be equipped with radio dispatching systems, although radios and GPS are already installed on all the buses, in case of emergencies. A central dispatching system with telephone operator(s) will need to be provided. Thus, the provision of a new product establishes a major change vector for Howes Bus Service and its IT department.

On the face of it, these two examples seem to be driven by completely different change vectors:

- The first example of ABC Inc. appears to show that customers' locations drives the change.

- The second example of Howes Bus Service appears to show that the company is chasing additional customers during the day to enhance or sustain the profitability of its total operations.

The commonality between these two examples, however, stems from changes in the same three external entities: Customers, Locations, and Products. In ABC's case, some existing customers have changed their Locations, thus making Location a barrier to expanding the customer base. ABC wants to expand their customer base by bringing their (same) Products to the Locations (actual or virtual) where their previous customers now live. As such, in ABC's case the Products remain the same, while the Customer and Locations have changed. In Howes' case, by changing the Product and offering it in slightly different Locations, Howes hopes to gain more customers in a different time period.

These actions are typical of dynamic businesses and the EA must reflect this, for the IT systems to be successful. Change vectors must therefore be a primary consideration when developing an EA.

CHAPTER 5

# How to Develop the New EA

In the previous chapters we have discussed the concepts and components of our enterprise architecture. In this chapter, we will address how to use these concepts and assemble these components into an enterprise architecture which will be dynamic, able to be used to cater for a changing environment, and able to predict change to a certain extent.

We first identify internal and external entities. We then identify relationships between internal and external entities, which are expressed through these entities' attributes. As discussed earlier, there are two types of relationships, one based on common values for the attributes – which are called *common value relationships* – and the other based on direct foreign key relationships – which are called *overt relationships*.

For *common value relationships*, we can then see that changes to values of those attributes of external entities will have a direct impact on the values needed for attributes of internal entities. Let's return to our previous example of a store's customers moving to more "upmarket" addresses away from the store's outlet. This causes a mismatch in the existing outlet's physical address and the physical addresses of its customers.

In this example, the external entity "customer" has an attribute of "address," as does the internal entity "store outlet." When we match these two attributes (customer address and store outlet address), it becomes clear that if many customers change their address attribute values (as they move away), the business will be impacted, because the two attributes are matched. We thus know the matched attributes, we know the change, and we know the change vector.

Another way of dealing with change is to link an external entity to an internal entity through *overt relationships*. When there was a new instance of an external entity, the organization would need to develop a new instance of the internal entity. One example already mentioned was the external entity Event, which linked to the internal entity Activity, through the overt relationship "triggers" (Event triggers Activity). When a new Event type was instantiated, a new Activity type (process) needed to be developed by the organization to deal with the new Event. We will also discuss this in more detail in this chapter.

When talking about the organization, it is useful to have a model of the organization available to reference. We will use the model we first introduced in Chapter 3. The approach we will use in this chapter is to base our discussion on this "three plus one" layered organization model and discuss each layer individually. We will start with the "plus one" Business Management layer, which will then unify the whole EA. As a refresher, this model is reproduced below.

Figure 8: The three-plus-one layered organization.

| Business Management | Customers & Product Sales |
| | Product Development & Product Build |
| | Suppliers & Supplies |

Please note that where computerized application systems are discussed, this also includes the relevant *business function*. For example, where a customer system is discussed, it includes the business function of attending to customer needs. Large organizations will have sophisticated application systems to help carry out the tasks involved with this, while smaller organizations will perform this manually.

# EA for business management

## Business intelligence

In a traditional hierarchically structured organization, Business Management acts as the "driver" of the whole organization, as well as managing the finances and personnel employed by the organization. We will look at what the driver needs, in the way of information, to effectively take the vehicle of the organization to where the driver wants to go. After that we will look at the other operational systems required to manage the finances and personnel for the business.

Essentially, the "driver" needs three groups of information:

- **Navigational group**. This is information associated with where the organization is currently compared to where it wants to be, and the "best way" of getting there.

- **Environmental group**. This is information associated with the organization's environment like road conditions, other road users, legal and associated conditions for travelling the road.

- **Internal conditions group**. This is information associated with the organization's performance and internal health.

Traditionally, the EA for Business Management has been focused on data warehousing or business intelligence solutions utilizing data about the internal conditions of the organization, with, in some cases, data from the environment like competitors' products and other external research data. However, in our new EA, we focus just as much on the external environment that the organization needs to operate in, as well as the internal environment of traditional EAs. Before we get into that discussion, consider the following diagram, Figure 9,which illustrates what the organization's "driver" should be getting.

At the bottom layer we have all the major entities, or Base Objects, that appear in a standard EA. These Base Objects appear wholly, or partly, in the organization's classical transaction processing systems. For example, the customer order management system would contain the Customer and Product Base Objects, and usually also the Customer Order sub-class of Event. Architects who build data warehouses will build all (or most) of the base objects into a single-view database, extracted, transformed, and loaded from transaction processing systems.

The next layer contains the Derived Objects, which are grouped abstractions of the Base Objects. "Customer Purchases" is a combination object of Customers by the Products they purchase via the Customer Orders they place. The Derived Objects will have a selection of the attributes from the Base Objects. Which attributes are selected for these depends largely on what the organization finds is useful and interesting for the Derived Objects. Architects familiar with data warehousing will be familiar with the Derived Object layer, as each object approximately corresponds to a data mart of a cube or multi-dimensional database.

Figure 9: Business Intelligence for Business Management.

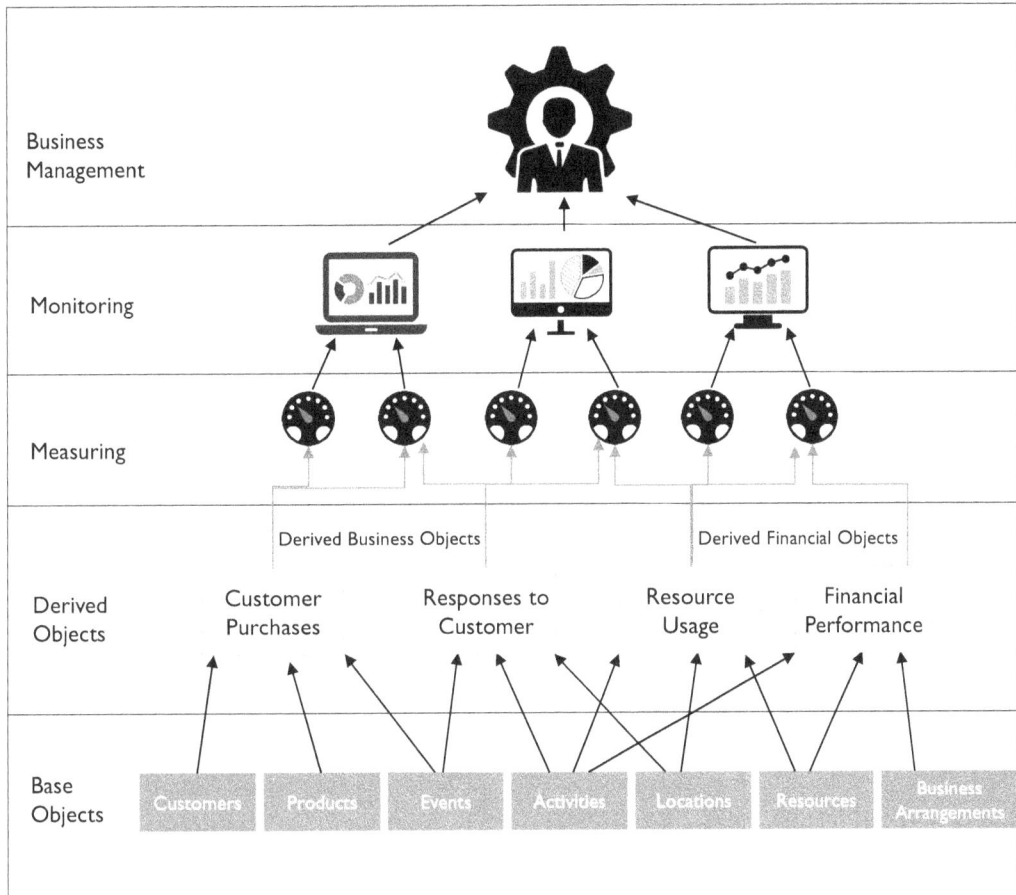

Figure 9: Business Intelligence for Business Management.

The Measuring layer represents the measurements or values taken at any one time, of selected attributes from the Derived Objects. These are attributes which are important to measure for the organization. In our vehicle example of the organization, this may represent speed, engine revolutions, or oil pressure at any instance in time. The key to understanding this is "at any instance in time." The Measuring layer contains the value of the attributes at a given *time slice*. This is the "dashboard" for the organization's performance. The individual attribute measurements may also contain warning or similar limits ("redlines") for each attribute. However, the important point to understand about this layer is that it shows values at a point in time.

The Monitoring layer is where the Measurement layer attribute values are shown over time. A time scale or period is selected, and the value of the attributes shown across this period. In this way any changes in these values can be easily seen, and trends identified. This kind of data is also known as "time series" data. Future directions for the values can also be predicted or surmised. This is the kind of information that the organization's managers want and need from their IT departments.

Finally, the top layer is where all this information is utilized and applied by the organization's management. The quality of this information obviously plays a key role in the quality of the decision-making carried out by management. That quality is therefore reliant on each layer below delivering accurate data.

In our previous simple example, where we matched the attribute "address" from the external entity "customer" and the internal entity "store outlet" in the base objects, we can see what a powerful tool this provides senior management. Even when rolled up into the Derived Objects, these attributes (or parts of them such as postal code) can be preserved, even when they become part of the Derived Objects such as "customer purchases." Senior management will be able to immediately see the trend of customers to live further from the "store outlet" location. This simple fact will probably trigger a rethink by management on the location of its "store outlet." Even if it doesn't, management will be aware that the change is occurring – which is usually not available to management in traditional EAs.

## Operational systems for managing the organization

The operational systems used in business management usually consist of the General Ledger and the Personnel and Payroll operational systems.

The Derived Financial Objects are found in the General Ledger system, which takes its feeds from several subsidiary systems. Derived Financial Objects, as discussed earlier, are abstract accounting-based views which usually contain one or more other objects, together with one or more of their attributes, to provide a general ledger item. The subsidiary feed systems to the General Ledger usually consist of:

- **Accounts Receivable (AR)**. This tracks the moneys owed *to* the organization. AR is sometimes synonymous with the customer billing system, but may not be; traditional AR systems may not provide all the functionality required by the customer-facing organization.

- **Accounts Payable (AP)**. This tracks the moneys owed *by* the organization to its suppliers and others. AP may also take some input feeds from the Payroll system.

- **Assets**. This tracks the values of the organization's assets (usually resources the organization uses to conduct its business) and thus its capital value. The Assets system usually identifies either individual high-value assets (like expensive machine tools, buildings, and computers), or classes of assets (like chairs and desks). Asset write-offs and write-downs are usually managed through this system.

The Personnel and Payroll operational system tracks who is employed by the organization and manages their pay. The "who is employed" includes permanent, temporary (contractors), and full and part-time employees. It usually holds personal details about each person employed, as well as their salary, seniority, performance, and other data related to the person's employment. The salary part includes all the periodic pay plus other payments like bonuses. Regular periodic payment advices are processed here and pay advices provided to the employees. The actual payment can be made directly to the employee's bank account or by check or cash.

## EA for customers and product sales

This is the customer facing part of the organization and typically has several key operational systems to support its business. This section discusses some of these possible key operational systems. However, when taking a more abstract or conceptual view, the systems used in the organization for its customer-facing (the top layer of the three-plus-one diagram) part are like those which would be used in its input requirements (the bottom layer of the three-plus-one diagram) part. The major differences are that the "customer" from the top layer becomes the "supplier" in the bottom layer. The "products" in the top layer are the organization's own products, while the "products" in the bottom layer are the suppliers' "products" (or supplies used as input for the organization's own products).

In the top layer we have a products system, while the bottom layer contains a supplies system. In the top layer we have a customer system, while in the bottom layer we have a supplier system. In the top layer we have an order management system for customers, but we also make orders to suppliers in the bottom layer. The parallels continue between top and bottom layer.

Having pointed out the similarities between top and bottom layers, the reader is cautioned against too much generalization because this may cause further downstream problems. These problems will usually come in the form of differing business rules, and thus possibly different actions and functionality, between customers and suppliers. In the accounting world the money owed *by* the customer is "accounts receivable" while the money owed *to* suppliers is "accounts payable," and the two have differing processes and rules.

For the purposes of this book, we will treat the systems required to support top and bottom layers of the organization separately.

In this top layer we are dealing with the following major data subject areas:

- **Products**. Those things the organization supplies to its customers

- **Customers**. A customer is really "a party playing the role of customer," so this is a specific role type for Party

- **Customer orders**. A type (or subtype) of Event – specifically a customer event

- **Customer accounts**. A specific type of Business Arrangement, whereby customers can obtain the product first and pay later or periodically

- **Locations**. Includes customer locations, locations of the organization's facilities, or any other place where the business interacts with customers

- **Business arrangements**. Ranges from legal responsibilities to warranties and standards around the products

The following section discusses the more important computerized application systems usually associated with this top layer of the organization.

## Product system

The Product or Product Catalog system lists all the organization's products, costs, and sales prices. It is often a part of another system such as sales or point of sales applications. Many telecoms organizations, for example, have several – one for each individual product (or product package).

Some organizations such as government departments and agencies have no Product or Product Catalog systems. This absence of a system (or too many systems) is due to a lack of clarity and unity as to what their product offerings are. Services provided to customers are also products, but these are often barely, or never, recognized as products. The process of developing a product system often assists the organization to clarify its own thinking about what products it offers to customers. A good product system should include the following major functions:

- Define anything provided to customers as a product, be that a widget, a service, or something more abstract, such as information.

- Distinguish between products (which could be provided separately to the customer) and features (like a car's color, which is a part of the car, but can't exist on its own, independent of the car).

- Treat a product package the same as a single item product. In other words, the system should *not* distinguish between standalone products and packages.

- Nest packages within other product packages. This is expressed as a normalization of a "many to many" containment or composed of, or included within relationship with the Product entity itself.

- Allow for the easy creation of new products, as well as the assembling of existing products into product packages.

- Allow for setting and changing the status of any individual product, feature, or product package. Common status values include "planned," "available," and "out of stock."

- Set different price types to be used against all products, features, and product packages. Price types include cost price, recommended retail price, wholesale price, and corporate price.

- Link different prices (and price types) to any product or feature, as well as apply different prices (and price types) to product packages. This is important because a price may be different than the sum of the component prices of the component packages.

- Allow for the creation of one-off (or "bespoke") product packages for any individual customer. This is especially important for service-focused organizations.

- Link to the order management system to show which products were supplied to which customer. This is essential for ongoing customer relationships, and is also important when a product is discontinued at the end of its lifecycle[20].

- Link to the activity management system, for those activities associated either with a service product or a physical product. This link is usually enabled through the Product Type to Activity Type relationship. [21]

- Link to the supplies system, to identify which product or feature components of each product were supplied by an external supplier.

- Link to the warehousing or stock management system to list where the product may be located, or where it could be supplied from.

- Link to the business arrangement system for warranties and legal requirements.

For organizations which provide mainly widgets (objects) as products putting together bespoke or one-off product packages for an individual customer, especially including at the point of sale, is an important advantage. However, for organizations which provide all of their products as services, it is essential to be able to tailor their product package for each customer. Hence for example, an

---

[20] Note that entity lifecycle analysis is not part of the discussion in this book but is pertinent to most EAs. It is assumed that lifecycle analysis would be done as part of any modeling activities in connection with the EA.

[21] Most well-managed organizations usually have a predefined set of actions/activity templates supporting any or all their product types. However, this may not be formalized if there is no activity or workflow management system in place.

IT consulting firm could put together a number of standard service products, make up some new service products, and offer these as a complete tailored product package to fulfill a specific customer's expressed requirements. A different customer may have a different package, based on that customer's different requirements.

## Customer system

The Customer system, often called a Customer Relationship Management (CRM) system, is more than a simple customer database, as this system will also need to record and track all customer interactions with the organization. Organizations whose customers are "cash and carry" customers, such as retail shops, may not have one of these. However, as an example, some large retail outlets selling high-end consumer goods do sometimes capture customer information, in the process of supplying add-on products such as extended warranties on their goods. Some of these organizations may in fact have customer systems, which they utilize to manage interactions with the customer, or to capture information about the customer. Organizations which also sell their products through internet channels usually need to capture customer data and thus should utilize a customer system.

Commercial organizations which do deploy customer systems are usually those whose customers are in a regular or long-term relationship with them, and commonly have accounts with the organization, or longer-term products like insurance policies. For those organizations which do deploy customer systems, the following major functions should be part of a good system:

- Ability to capture the basics about the customer, as well as verify some of this data (like address and phone numbers). This information must be easily updated, in a verifiable and secure way, to ensure the data is current.

- Ability to set and change the status of individual customers. Statuses such as "good" and "long term/time" are commonly used.

- Ability to link a customer to credit rating data about that customer, where appropriate. Credit rating data about customers must be secure and up to date.

- Ability to build organizational hierarchies, as well as personnel hierarchies (i.e., who works for whom), about the customer.

- Ensure tight security on customer data.

- Record all interactions with the customer, including phone and personal interactions. Also record any undertakings such as promises of action, and pass this to an activity management system.

- Link to the order management system to capture new customer data and update existing customer data.

- Link to the product system to capture which product the customer acquired. This is especially important when it comes to warranties (Business Arrangements), product recalls and/or support, as well as when planning product phase-outs (end of product life-cycle).

## Order system

The Order Management system is at the front end of the organization's interactions with a customer. A good order management system should include the following functions:

- Link to the product system to select the standard product that the customer wants, together with the pricing for that product.

- Functionality to allow point-of-sale personnel to customize products where necessary, and within a rules base, for individual customers.

- Functionality to allow point-of-sale personnel to customize product pricing within the rules allowed by the organization, for each customer.

- Functionality to move the Product Type into an interim "ordered products" folder and reduce stock holdings of the product.

- Functionality to take the "ordered products" from the interim folder to the final "sold products" folder.

- Links *to* the activity management system, where the actions taken are to provide the product (provisioning the product) or, if the product is a service product, to initiate the service through initiating and instantiating the activities.

- Links *from* the activity management system, so that the actions taken can be tracked. These may take the form of scheduled milestones, helping to keep the customer informed of the progress of their order.

- Ability to set and change status of the order. If the order is for complex products, or for more than one product, these may not necessarily be delivered at the same time.

- Links to the account management and billing system, to initiate account setup, updates, billing, and payment for the ordered products by the customer.

- Links to the Sold Product system, to record the product as sold, and to record details of the product instance (such as serial number).

Note that the "Links to the Sold Product" system can in fact be a part of the Products system. Some organizations hold the data about sold products only in their customer account and billing system, but this is not recommended given the possible downstream issues with business arrangements such as warranties on the product and post-purchase servicing. In other words, the sold product exists as an entity in its own right and may have a number of distinct business processes associated with it. As such, the sold product should not be held, if possible, in the customer accounts system. However, it is perfectly reasonable for "controlled copies" of the sold product to be stored there.

## Customer billing system

In some industries, notably the telecommunications industry, the customer account and billing system is treated as the core of its portfolio of computerized systems. This is so often the case that a huge amount of functionality like order management and customer contact is often crammed into this system, making it extremely unwieldy to manage, let alone modify. Likewise, many of these systems in the past could only cope with a small set of product types, usually only those the organization sold at the time of their acquisition, thus often making it impossible to add new products or customize products for individual customers. This commonly resulted in the organization not being flexible enough to cater to what their customers really wanted, and thus become uncompetitive. A good customer billing system should do the following:

- Bill for any existing product or additional new products, either as continued periodic billing or one-off charges. In the telecommunications industry, for instance, there is often a fixed installation charge plus additional usage charges every month.

- Charge the correct price, from a range of price types, as agreed with the customer.

- Set or change a billing cycle, as agreed to with the customer.

- "Roll up" billing or periodic statements for all accounts belonging to individual customers in accordance with that customer's requirements, or that customer's organizational hierarchy.

- Link to the customer system, for different roles, such as the account owner and the contact person for the account.

- Link from order management system for completed orders and products, as well as agreed sales price. Depending on business rules, some items on a partially completed order may commence billing before the total order is completed.

- Link to product system for sold products, as well as pricing and changes to the pricing of existing sold products.

- Link from the activity management system for billable activities. If an installation activity is priced on an hourly basis, this indicates the number of actual hours to be billed.

- Link from the resource system for billable resources. For instance, if an installation includes materials, these may be billed to the customer.

- Link with the general ledger accounts receivable.

- For organizations like telecommunications companies, link from the "rating engine," or equivalent, which calculates the price of ongoing usage products (such as calls or data used).

## Event system

An outward-looking organization needs to have a structured way of dealing with events that impact either the whole organization or parts of it. Some routine or regularly occurring events, such as customer orders, are dealt with through dedicated systems. Other events are not, and this section proposes a system to do just that – deal with non-regular events in an Event system.

Although this system could be placed either in the top customer-facing layer, or in the middle product-building layer, we have chosen to place this in the top layer, the most outward-looking layer of the organization. Events which affect the organization are often drawn to attention by external people or organizations (external parties). What we are talking about here is an event reporting and classification system, with additional capabilities to be discussed below.

As defined earlier, an event is something which occurs outside the organization's control, and to which the organization needs to respond. Some examples of non-regular events have already been provided. Such events usually come to an organization's attention in the following ways:

- A customer contacts the organization, perhaps due to some problems or queries with their products.

- A person who is not a customer contacts the organization, perhaps inquiring about products.

- Another organization contacts the organization.

- Unusual performance is reported by instrumentation on one or more of the organization's resources (an "alarm" is triggered).

- An entity, whether external or internal, reports a problem with respect to business arrangements, like compliance with some undertaking or legal requirement.

Effectively, the event system holds the organization's "memory and experience" data. A good event system should include the following functions:

- Record the details, including contact details, of the person or organization making the event report.

- Record all relevant details about the event at the time of reporting. Allow for additional details to be recorded at a later stage.

- Classify the event by any existing pre-classified event types. If there is doubt about the type of event, allow later classification to either existing event types, or a newly-created event type.

- Linking of event types to activity type templates. This will instantiate the relevant activity template when an event of that type is recorded. It will also provide immediate feedback as to what will happen next and when.

- Through the event type – activity type link, trigger the relevant activity type template to be instantiated.

- Through the event instance – activity instance link, enable a view of progress through the instantiated activities, especially milestone activities.

- Link the reported event to any resource used by the organization.

- Link the reported event to any product provided by the organization, including the customer to whom the product was provided.

- Link the reported event to any supplier to the organization.

- Link the reported event with any personnel or employee within the organization.

- Link the reported event to any location where it may have occurred, if relevant.

# EA for product development and build

This middle layer/tier of the three-plus-one organizational model is the engine room or factory for the organization. This tier is involved with the development and build of the organization's products, using input managed by the bottom tier, and supplying and supporting products sold in the top tier. Essentially, in this tier the organization takes products from its suppliers, and adds its own inputs to provide products to its customers. This is the case even if the suppliers' products are not actually transformed. For example, a retail store which sells household appliances adds value by bringing together many different brands of the same type of product, such as televisions, into the same display space such as the shop itself, where customers can compare them. The retail shop may even add further value to the product through providing in-house warranties (business arrangements) on the products, over and above what the manufacturer provides.

Many have treated this tier as the most important part of their organization, and thus invested heavily in it. Its relative importance would certainly depend on the type of activities and products that the organization is involved in producing.

The major data subject areas used in this tier are:

- **Resources**. These are all the things (like machinery, vehicles, buildings, and ICT, but not people) used to transform products from the organization's suppliers into products the organization provides to its own customers.

- **Activities**. These are all the things people in the organization do to produce the products. Note that some activities can also be performed by computer systems.

- **Business Arrangements**. These are those things like laws, contracts, and standards.

- **Employees** (parties in the role of employees and managers, for example). These are the people with the skills required to produce the products using the input products and the organization's resources.

The following discusses the more important computerized application systems usually associated with this middle layer of the organization.

## Resource system

The Resource system can be the inventory of all things which are used by the organization, such as buildings, vehicles, machinery, ICT, desks, and chairs, depending on the organization and its business. In reality, the only inventories considered are those of things used to develop or build the organization's products. The complete record of the organization's resources is usually held in the accounting function's assets register.

Depending on the organization's activities and products, not all organizations would use a resource system. For example, a legal office providing legal *service* products to their customers may not use such a system. On the other hand, a vehicle manufacturing organization with many machine tools as well as robots may have a great need for such a system, as it keeps track of resources used or assigned to make each product. A telecoms organization would find it essential to have a resource system for its network elements, as these are assigned and configured to provide the products for its customers. Sometimes those assignments and configurations are done through software in the resource system interfacing directly to the software controlling the actual resource.

A solid, comprehensive resource management system should include the following:

- The ability to describe resources in terms of purpose, capability, purchase cost, and any upgrades or maintenance required.

- A way for managers to assign tasks or products to individual resources, or groups of resources, and vice versa. This is achieved through links with the activity management, products, and orders systems. This also allows the business to link products with the resources used to produce them.

- A way to set and change the status of each resource, in order to manage that resource's availability and maintenance.

- Links to any events (like breakdowns) that have affected each resource.

- Links to the activity management system, to assign resources to other activities (such as maintenance activities associated with the resource).

- Links with the asset system within the general ledger system. Note that there may not be a one-to-one relationship between a resource and an asset.

## Activity system

Sometimes known as the workflow management system, the Activity system (or activity management system) allows for the definition of tasks or activities to be performed, and their assignment to employees or staff of the organization to carry out. Activities can also be automated, so a good activity system should also be able to trigger these computerized activities.

Activity systems are important because they assist the organization to cost effectively standardize its processes in response to most expected events, especially those events which occur regularly (such as customer orders). Standardization of processes is also at the heart of many standards specifications (like the ISO 9000 series), under which many organizations seek accreditation. For organizations that exclusively provide service products, even if every service is customized for each customer (like in consulting firms, for instance), standardized processes can be leveraged to ensure quality and predictability. It is possible to determine the cost of a standard process for both time and money, after which prices for customers can be set.

Any activity within a process flow can consist of other activities as a complete sub-process. Even customized service activities can be built up from standardized sub-activities. The usefulness of an activity system to an organization lies in how well it's been configured for its processes, and how well it's been used for products developed for customers.

Furthermore, decision type activities which allow branching of the process based on the results of a decision, provide for sophisticated processes to be developed and configured. Decision type activities are usually framed as a question, with binary (yes or no) outcomes; in special circumstances, trinary (yes, no, or a third possibility like "unknown") outcomes could be catered to. Often workflow management systems build these into their functionality and call them a "business rules engine," providing a series of yes/no branches.

A good activity system should include the following functions:

- Define individual activity types including name, description, comments (including instructions), expected minimum, most likely, and maximum effort or time to carry out the activity, and associated costs to carry out the activity

- Define milestone type activities, which do not have an effort or duration, but are markers along the activity chain process.

- Define relationships between activities, including start-start, finish-start, and finish-finish. This strings the activities together as a process flow.

- Include decision type activities and allow branch on "yes" and branch on "no" relationships with other "doing" or decision activity types.

- Loop back to an earlier activity from one of the branches in the decision type activity. This allows the inclusion of quality checking activities.

- Instantiate activity type chains (i.e. processes) into actual activities, based on some trigger like a customer order. Each activity instance needs to inherit the activity type's name, description, and comments.

- Calculate earliest and latest start and finish dates (based on the expected minimum and maximum effort time for the equivalent activity types), regularly update these calculations based on changing work conditions, and assign each calculated timeframe to each activity within the process.

- The accountable person must be able to modify parts of the predefined end-to-end process, by inserting or deleting activities from a process, as warranted by particular circumstances.

- The accountable party should easily be able to make a decision by selecting the desired branch through the yes/no response. These deletions should be reversible as needed.

- Define completely new "bespoke" processes (linked sets of activities), and insert these anywhere within predefined processes.

- Link to the product system, allowing product types to be linked to activity types.

- Link to the customer Order system. The activity system can link to the order system in one of two ways. The first way is a link from the Product System via product types to their equivalent activity types to instantiate those activity types into activities for the ordered product type. The second important link is feedback within the customer Order system to expose the relevant milestone activities.

- Link to the employees and resources systems. Each activity should be assigned to the appropriate personnel and physical resources needed.

- The person assigned to each activity must be able to record the actual start and finish date and time for that activity.

## Business arrangements system

The Business Arrangement system is essentially a text-based reference database of all the various types of agreements – legal, contractual, standards-based, or otherwise. Given the complexity of the modern commercial environment, a good Business Arrangements system repays its investment very quickly. A good Business Arrangements system should include the following major functions:

- Store electronic or scanned documents in the usual standard formats (DOC, DOCX, or PDF), and make them available to be read partially, or entirely, using the usual desktop tools.

- Control the versions of all documents which are stored.

- Classify documents by type and content.

- Attach keywords (and other search criteria) to enable rapid location of unstructured information contained in the documents.

- Search and retrieve any document, or part of a document, using popular search methods and paradigms.

- Allow all or parts of a document to be linked to any other object instance (or object type, or person) in any other system. For example, a warranty document is part of a business arrangement type, and the two need to be linked.

## Employees system

The Employees system is not the Personnel Payroll system previously discussed, but is linked to that system. The Employees system provides assignment and management of employees' work. Not all organizations use such a system. But for larger organizations that work on a project basis (rather than, say, a production line), this kind of system is extremely useful. A good Employees system should be able to:

- Record relevant employees' personal details and synchronize these with the Personnel Payroll system.

- Record all employees' skills and experience in a structured way.

- Match employees' skills and experience to those demanded by activities within process flows.

- Record and manage employee availability and work times.

- Summarize employee activity assignments from the past, including completed activities.

- Link to the Activity system, allowing employees to be assigned to activities within process chains. Self-checking should ensure that the employee is not over- or double-allocated.

- Link to the Products system, to identify employees associated with certain products (either as sales people, or in their development, for instance).

- Link to the Customer system, identifying employees associated with customers. The two most common types of such associations are when the employee *is* also the customer, or when the employee is responsible for or in contact with the customer.

- Link to the Order system to identify employees associated with customer orders. One example may be that of a returning customer's request to get help from a specific employee they know and trust.

- Link to the Resources system to identify employees associated with individual resources. For example, if an employee has been issued a company cell phone, they must be linked to that particular resource instance.

- Link to the Business Arrangement system to identify employees associated with individual business arrangements, such as an employment contract.

## Manufacturing system

Although the Manufacturing system is the core system where the organization physically builds or makes its product, it is uniquely tied to each individual organization and specialized to its products.

For example, if the organization manufactures something, then this system may very well comprise the collective IT and associated robotics used in that process. On the other hand, if the organization conducts research using input information which is then analyzed, and output as reports, the IT used for "manufacturing" will probably be of an analytical nature. Furthermore, IT service organizations commonly utilize software tools on their clients' sites to develop software to the clients' specifications such as CASE tools, analytical tools, and code generators. In some cases, there may not be any system "manufacturing" the organization's products, as these may all be manually made by its skilled personnel.

The manufacturing system can be either exclusively IT-controlled, running a mix of IT and manual processes, or comprise exclusively manual processes. Examples of each of these include:

- Telecommunication networks are nowadays entirely run by "intelligent network elements," which can be configured and commanded remotely through interfaces with other IT systems (e.g. the Resource system). Manual work is generally confined to some network configuration, such as manually connecting wires, maintenance, and construction.

- Car manufacturing is often a combination of robotic elements stamping out predesigned parts, and manual processes carried out by the organization's personnel.

- Legal services are often all provided through the organization's personnel, with minimum use of IT beyond desktop word processing and looking up references from digitized libraries.

The manufacturing system, then, is the component that really gives an EA its unique identity. Most of the other systems discussed in this chapter are common across most organizations, with some variations. The manufacturing system, though, will be quite different from one organization to the next. As enterprise architects, we must remain aware that this manufacturing system exists at the core of the organization. It must be handled with great care, especially when linking this critical system to all the other systems. These links, after all, form part of the total picture which must be drawn for the EA to be complete.

## EA for suppliers and supplies

This bottom tier of the three-plus-one organizational model is the supplier-facing part of the organization, which has many similarities (in terms of functions and operational systems) as the EA for customers and product sales in the top tier. The functions and systems of the supplier-facing layer tend to be a mirror image (or reversal) of those in the customer- and product-facing layers. Instead of products being produced and supplied to customers, the organization itself becomes the customer for others' products, which it then uses to produce its own products.

This supplier-facing bottom layer comprises the following data subject areas:

- **Supplies** (also called Suppliers' Products) are the outputs of *other* organizations; they become the supplies and inputs for this organization in question.

- **"Suppliers"** is a specific role type for a Party, literally described as "a party in the role of a supplier."

- **"Supplier order"** is a type of Event – specifically an Event triggered by an internal Activity. One classic case is when inventory for some part falls below a predefined number and triggers a series of activities to reorder the part.

- **Supplier accounts**. An organization keeps these accounts to track how much money they owe to each of their suppliers.

- **Locations**. These can be supplier locations, or locations for the organization's establishments (e.g., warehouses and manufacturing plants).

- **Business arrangements**. Some familiar examples are supplier contracts and warranties, through to supply chain requirements such as fair work practices to be implemented by suppliers, and standards to be applied to supplier products.

In the following sections, we will discuss the important application systems usually associated with this bottom tier of an organization.

## Supplies system

The Supplies system is basically the top layer's Products system, with the difference being that the products held in the Supplies system are products which the organization purchases or obtains from other organizations, either for its own use as consumable products, or as resources, or services, or to package together with its own input products. These supplies are used to produce, or help produce the products which the organization provides to its customers.

Like the Products system, the Supplies system needs to be able to deal with both physical things, as well as services products from other organizations, and different types and levels of pricing from the supplier organizations. The Supplies system also needs to be able to hold information about similar supplies from different suppliers, and to hold information about supplies which are required/needed but not currently available like left-handed screwdrivers. A good Supplies system should include the following major functions:

- Define anything as a supply, including a physical item, a service, or something abstract like information.

- Distinguish between supplies which can be bought separately, and features of supplies which "describe" supplies but are not provided separately from the supplies, such as color.

- Treat standalone supplies and packages of supplies in exactly the same way. As with the Product system, sometimes one supply can belong to multiple supply packages, or a supply package can be comprised of multiple smaller supply packages.

- Allow for the easy creation of new supply specifications, as well as the assembling of supplies into supply packages.

- Allow for the setting and changing of status on any supply, supply package, or supply feature.

- Set different price types for any supply, supply package, or supply feature.

- Link to the supplies ordering system to show which supplies have been ordered.

- Link to the supplier system to identify which supply is provided by what supplier.

- Link to the stock warehousing or inventory system (if used) to identify where the supplies are to be received or stored.

- Link to the business arrangement system for warranty, contractual, and legal requirements.

## Supplier system

Like its twin Customer system, the Supplier system is much more than a simple database of supplier details. This system must record and track the organization's interactions with suppliers (calling them "supplier events"), as well as other noteworthy details about suppliers. An important development in the past two decades is that a company's own reputation can in fact be impacted by the reputation of its suppliers, e.g. with the supplier's behavior to their own workers.

One example of this is in the fashion industry, where clothes are often manufactured in low labor-cost countries, and those manufacturers' working conditions and pay to their workers are below internationally acceptable norms. This in turn could affect the organization's sales and performance within its chosen environment. Thus "supply chain management" is often becoming more than managing the provision of the correct supplies at the right time.

Another aspect of supply chain management is the quality of the supplies which are components in the organization's own products. An organization is accountable for its products (including all their components) – whether they were made by that organization or a different supplier. As such, any warranties (i.e., business arrangements), that the organization provides to its customers for its products, would usually have equivalent warranties with suppliers for supply components that go into those products.

For purposes of the EA, warranties that come with supplies require us to link business arrangements in that system to the suppliers and their supplies which were used in this organization's products. Supplies from direct suppliers could of course also include components from another, indirect supplier. However, whether this one (or more) removed in the supply chain is of importance to this organization, would depend on the individual circumstances of the organization. That issue will not be explored here.

For a good supplier system, the following major functions should be included:

- Capture the basic details (e.g., name, address, phone numbers) of the supplier, and verify the accuracy of this data.

- Securely update this supplier data as needed.

- Link a supplier to financial information (like market capitalization, credit ratings, and other relevant business information about the supplier).

- Build organizational hierarchies (sometimes called "organizational structures") and personnel hierarchies (i.e. charts that show who works for whom) within the supplier.

- Ensure tight security on supplier data. This data is equivalent to the organization's customer data and needs to be treated in a secure manner.

- Record interactions with the supplier, including phone and personal interactions. Also record any promises of action, either by the supplier or the organization.

- Link to the activity management system, feeding records of interactions as appropriate.

- Link to the supplies ordering system to capture new supplier data and update existing supplier data.

- Link to the supplies system to capture which supplies are supplied by the supplier.

- Link to the business arrangement system to identify what business arrangements (like warranties and contracts) apply to each supplier.

## Supplies ordering system

The Supplies Ordering system is at the front end of the organization's interactions with its suppliers, whether the supplies obtained are incorporated into its own products, or deployed as resources, or used as consumable items to enable the organization to operate efficiently. Not *all* supplies are ordered through this system. For example, petty cash-based purchases and minor office cash expenses may not be processed here, but may be lumped together under miscellaneous minor expenses in the accounting systems.

A good supplies ordering system should include the following major functions:

- Link to the supplies system to select the pre-defined, regularly-used supplies that the organization wants.

- Link to the business arrangement system, allowing users to review contracts and agreements.

- Move the ordered supplies type (similar to the Product Type) into an interim "ordered supplies" folder, pending final delivery of the supplies to the organization.

- Move the "ordered supplies" from the interim folder to the final "completed purchase" folder when appropriate.

- Link to the warehousing system, providing data about which supplies are to be delivered to what warehouse.

- Link to the activity management system to trigger relevant actions. If external services are ordered, this may also require the organization's personnel to perform some activities with respect to those providing the services.

- Link from the activity management system to expose the progress of the process, usually through milestones achieved, to the person who placed the order.

- Set and change the status of an order.

- Link to the supplier accounts system. This allows initiation of payments to the supplier, either at order completion or progressively.

## Supplier accounts system

Like the customer accounts system, the Supplier Accounts system links to the supplier orders system and tracks from what was ordered to what needs to be paid to suppliers. Essentially the accounts payable system for the organization, the supplier accounts system would also link to the business arrangement system for contract and quotation pricing of supplies that have been ordered, as well as terms of payment. When suppliers send in their invoices, these can be checked against the amounts held for supplies from contract or quotation prices. A good supplier accounts system should have the following feature functions:

- Record any supply purchased and recurring supplies billed periodically (like utilities). Record the correct prices from a range of prices agreed with the supplier, as well as apply any discounts agreed to in business arrangements.

- The system should be easily audited, including transparency and traceability, to provide evidence of accurate billing and payments.

- Link to the supplies ordering system, to pass read-only data about completed and partially completed orders and agreed prices.

- Link to the supplier system, to pass read-only data containing full details of each supplier for each supplier account.

- Link to the general ledger accounts payable system, to update outstanding, pending, and completed payments to suppliers.

## Warehousing and inventory system (optional)

Not all organizations have or need a Warehousing and Inventory system. These are usually used by organizations that deal with physical objects as supplies (i.e., objects that are included in or become their products). Thus, an organization whose only product consists of services is unlikely to require one of these systems. Inventory is *what* supplies are available for the manufacturing of products, and *what* products are available for supply to customers. Warehousing, on the other hand, is *where* those supplies and products are located. So, inventory is about the *what*, and warehousing is about the *where* – both of supplies and products. The two are often interlinked or contained in the one system.

A warehouse is conceptually a place where both the organization's supplies or products may be stored, before they are used or sold respectively. It can range from a sophisticated building with robotic handling/storage of goods to an open-air car park where finished cars await transport to other places. An inventory system essentially tracks what is in the warehouse (what comes in and what goes out), so that whether the item is a supply or a product, it can be made available for its end use as quickly and efficiently as practicable, while the warehousing system tracks precisely where the inventory item is located.

Because of the variety of warehousing and inventory systems available and used by various organizations, this book will not go into any detail about this system. Enterprise architects however, need to be aware of these kinds of systems, and how they can assist the organization in efficiently and cost effectively produce their products and provide those products to their customers. There is certainly a lot of information available in existing literature on how these systems operate, and how they can link in with other systems to enhance the organization's operations.

Just like manufacturing systems, warehousing and inventory systems tend to be specific to each organization that uses them, the products they provide, and the industries they are involved in. We will therefore not discuss details about these systems. However, a good warehousing and inventory system will need to include:

- Links with the customer order system and/or the supplies ordering system.

- Links with the supplies and product systems.

- Links with the manufacturing system.

## Complete systems architecture

Having covered a lot of ground in terms of what systems are likely and where in our EA, this section will put this all into context, starting with the diagram below. Figure 10 is an overview of the common systems architecture components, showing the systems or applications that most organizations share, as well as the ones they don't necessarily share, as discussed in the previous sections. Please note that smaller organizations may not deploy all these systems. However, they will have equivalent manual processes, utilizing essentially the same data in the same data subject areas as described here.

Based on the earlier 3-plus-one model of the organization, we have inserted the computerized systems or business applications into the tiers as described in the previous sections of this chapter. These are color and shape coded for easy reading, thus:

- Yellow boxes represent the applications likely to be found in the top "Customers and Products" tier of the organization.

- Green boxes represent the applications likely to be found in the middle "Product development and Product Build" tier of the organization.

- Blue boxes represent the applications likely to be found in the bottom "Suppliers and Supplies" tier of the organization.

- Turquoise boxes represent the applications likely to be found in the vertical "Business Management" tier of the organization.

Figure 10: Common Systems Architecture components.

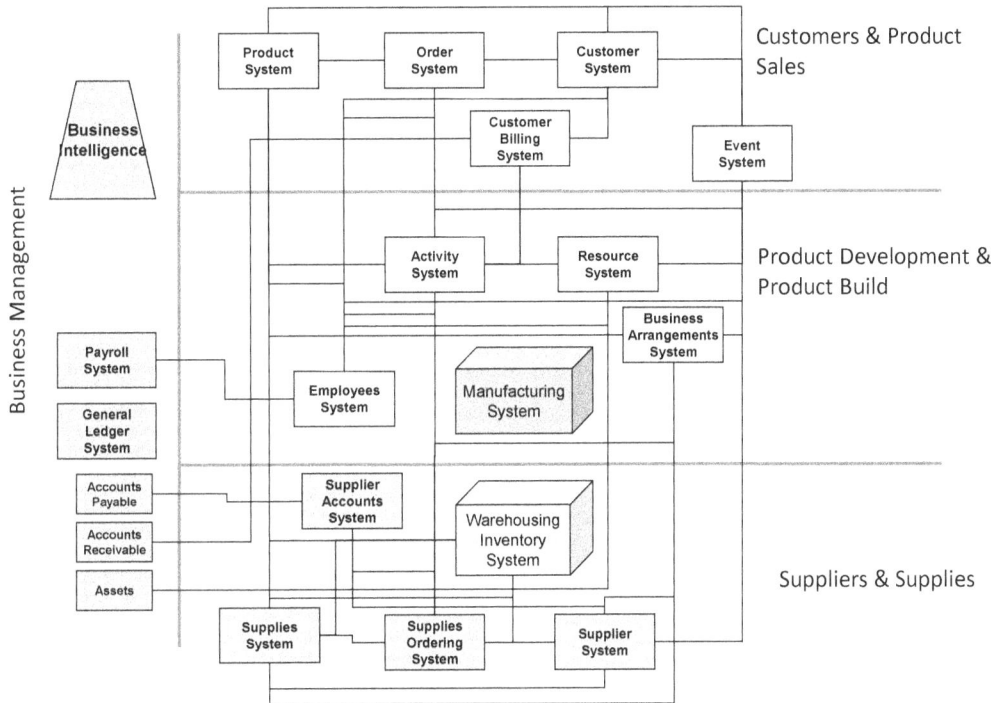

This leaves the pink box labeled "Manufacturing System" and the orange box labeled "Warehousing Inventory System" as being organization-specific applications, shown as three-dimensional boxes in the diagram. As mentioned in the previous sections, these two "systems" are very much tailored to each organization, depending on what the organization does.

However, this is a very much "inside-out" view of most organizations' applications architecture. This book is about the "outside-in" view as well, placing the organization into its environment and viewing the environmental factors which impinge on the organization, and in which the organization has to operate. To do this we have taken the same picture as above, shrunk it slightly, and added the major environmental entities, as well as the internal entities.

The internal and environmental entities were already discussed in Chapter 4, so we will simply list these below. The environmental entities are:

- Products – Organization's
- Party – Customers
- Events
- Locations
- Business Arrangements
- Products – Supplies
- Party – Suppliers

The internal entities are:

- Activities
- Resources
- Party – Personnel
- Derived Objects (derived from every other entity – see the earlier discussion on Business Intelligence)

Figure 11 summarizes the total picture for the EA in terms of business applications and the data subject areas they address. The environmental entities are shown as blue ovals, while the internal entities are shown as orange ovals. There is a bit of repetition because, as previously discussed, Supplies are a class of Product which the organization obtains from other organizations and uses for input, and Suppliers are a Party in the role of suppliers to the organization. Therefore, Suppliers and Customers are really two parts of the same Party entity, while Products and Supplies are really two parts of the Product entity.

The data used by the business applications systems comes from the environmental and internal subject area entities, shown in the oval shapes in

Figure 11, so lines between the systems and those ovals are not drawn for the purposes of simplicity. Instead, the data used by the business applications systems was described in some detail in the earlier sections of this chapter. However, those links are shown in the matrix table below Table 1.

Figure 11: Common Systems Architecture components and subject areas.

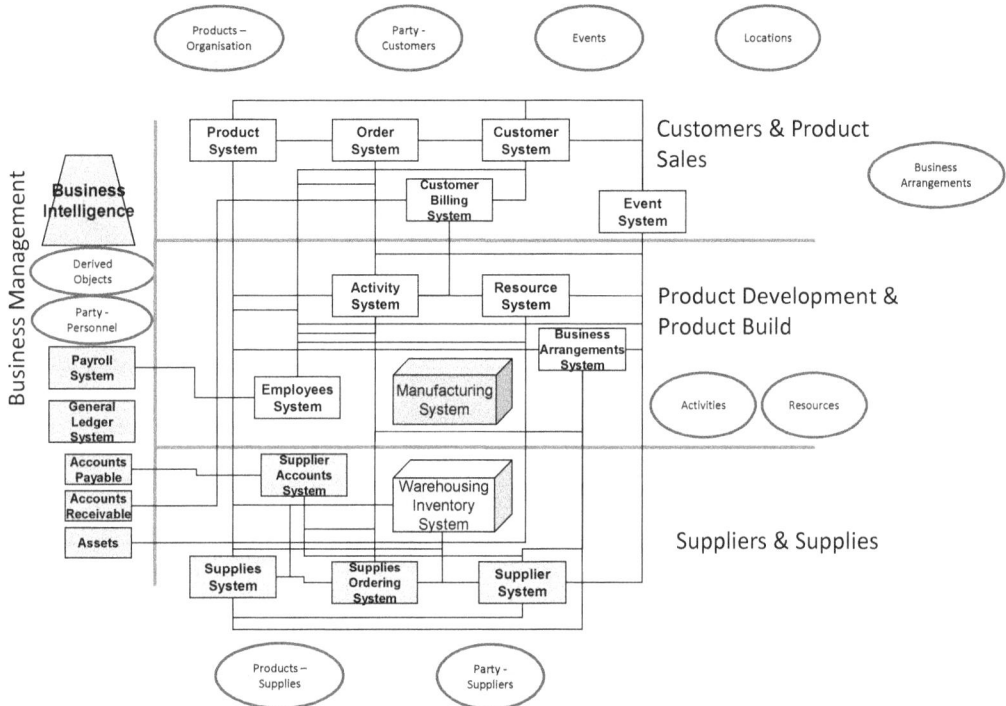

The data subject areas are the columns, with headers color-coded in a similar fashion to the above diagrams. Derived Objects appears as both a data subject area in the end column, and an application in the bottom row, because it consists of derived objects (data plus process) from all the other subject areas.

Table 1. Matrix of Application Systems Using Data from Subject Areas.

| Entity Subject Area (Application using Entity) | Product System | Order System | Customer System | Customer Billing System | Event System | Activity System | Resource System | Business Arrangements System | Employees System | Manufacturing System | Supplies System | Supplies Ordering System | Supplier System | Supplier Accounts System | Warehousing Inventory System | General Ledger System | Accounts Payable | Accounts Receivable | Assets | Payroll System | Business Intelligence | Derived Objects |
|---|---|---|---|---|---|---|---|---|---|---|---|---|---|---|---|---|---|---|---|---|---|---|
| Party – Customer | | Y | Y | Y | Y | Y | | Y | Y | ? | | | | | | | | Y | | | | Y |
| Party – Suppliers | | | | | | Y | | Y | | ? | Y | Y | Y | Y | | | Y | | | | | Y |
| Party - Personnel | | | | | | Y | Y | | Y | ? | | | | | | | | | | Y | | Y |
| Product – Organisation | Y | | Y | Y | Y | Y | Y | Y | Y | ? | | | | | Y | Y | | Y | | | | Y |
| Product – Supplies | Y | | | | | Y | | Y | | ? | Y | Y | Y | | Y | Y | | | | | | Y |
| Events | | | | | Y | | Y | | | ? | | | | | | | | | | | | Y |
| Locations | Y | | | | | | Y | | | ? | Y | | | | Y | | | | | | | Y |
| Business Arrangements | Y | | | Y | Y | Y | | Y | Y | ? | Y | Y | | | | | | | | | | Y |
| Activities | Y | Y | | Y | Y | Y | Y | | Y | ? | Y | | | | | Y | | | | Y | | Y |
| Resources | | | | | Y | Y | Y | | | ? | | | | | | | | | Y | | | Y |
| Derived Objects | | | | | | | | | | ? | | | | | | | | | | | Y | |

What then does all this mean? From the discussion to this point, we can reasonably draw several conclusions. One is that organizations *share* similar business applications systems. The detail of what they do and how they do it may vary, but basically the functionality is similar. In our organism analogy, a liver from a cow has similar functions to the liver from a fish, or a cat. It can also be concluded that organizations do *not* share two basic areas of business applications: their manufacturing system(s) and their warehousing system(s). These are specific to what the organization does.

Every organization may not necessarily have the range of business applications depicted above and described earlier in this chapter, because their size or complexity may not warrant it. However, someone within the organization will be carrying out functions like the depicted and described business applications systems – some of these may be purely manual processes. For example, it may be extremely unlikely that a single-operator business will need a CRM system, because the number of customers it has may not warrant it, but the business operator still carries out the work of that system as part of their daily business activities.

Some organizations may outsource some of the functions depicted or described in this chapter. For small organizations, personnel, payroll, and accounting are commonly outsourced to specialized service providers, as this provides them with efficient or cost-beneficial "back-office" services. The problem with an outsourcing model however is that gaps appear in the organization's knowledge of its own world, which are often not immediately apparent or covered by those service providers. Outsourcing in this way is like taking away some of the instruments or sensors or controls normally provided in a car like the fuel gauge. Unless the organization is aware of the missing bits, it could lead to unforeseen consequences.

Some organizations are simply unaware of what the complete picture looks like. Without a clear idea of what they should be striving for, and what they need to address the gaps, organizations fall into the trap of "not knowing what you don't know". Developing BI solutions and management reporting is one method of discovering some of these knowledge gaps. Developing an EA is a more thorough way of covering all these, as the EA should also provide possible solutions to filling both the knowledge gaps and developing IT capability where needed.

In summary, this chapter describes the environment that all organizations need to operate in, as well the "internal organs" that it needs to operate in that environment. That said, this chapter has also highlighted the commonality between all organizations in what they require in the way of "internal organs," as well as what is distinct between different types of organizations. In the following chapters we will examine the implications of this, as well as look at some non-obvious cases.

## More about change

Now that we have established the general picture of the complete systems architecture in our new EA, the following provides two more examples of how we could use this to deal with the impacts of change. Change may come in many forms, so trying to categorize or describe all types of change would be futile. We will instead try, with these simple examples, to show how our new EA could be used to rapidly ascertain impacts that can be followed up later for more detailed investigation.

### Example 1 – a new type of event

The organization has been made aware of a data breach to its customer database (i.e. an Event), whereby hackers have been able to obtain details about its customers. There is no process (i.e. series of Activities) in place to define the response, and how the organization will deal with this new type of Event, given that this is the first time it has occurred. Accordingly, it is a change the organization must respond to. Referring to Figure 11, we might take the following steps:

1.  If an Event system existed, we would need to define this new type and instance of this event in that system.

2.  If an Activity system existed, management would need to work out the activity steps (process) to respond to it. We would probably record this process (activity steps) as a new Activity Type template, and link it to the new Event type, so that if that type of event occurs again, we will have a ready-made process to follow. We would instantiate this template and start allocating individual activity steps to individual persons or positions within the organization to carry out each activity. This would be done through the Activity system's links to the Employee system, if that exists (otherwise that may be a manual process).

3.  If there are insufficient skilled personnel within the organization itself to perform the necessary forensic and other work related to the data breach, we may need to go to an outside organization or individuals for assistance. This will probably entail using the Supplier, Supplies Ordering, and Supplies systems to obtain the necessary service products.

4.  Now we can examine the actual break-in Event in some detail. We can see that there may be greater impacts involved with the data breach than just the Customer data. The reason for this is that the Customer system has many links to other systems, which may have been used by those perpetrating the customer data breach. Presumably these will need to be checked and followed by the forensic work. Thus, with this road map, we can already determine the scope of work required to be carried out by the forensic and other teams, assigned to this event.

Obviously, experts in IT security and others more experienced in this area will be able to describe further work and steps needed to respond to this event. However, the point here is that our new EA can be used to ascertain very quickly the nature, scope, and extent of the response needed to this new type of event.

## Example 2 – new or changed legislation

A retail sales chain organization has been made aware that changes in legislation covering some consumer items now require that those items include additional tests and checks, as well as additional labelling. The purpose of the new laws is to bring these items, which people consume, into line with other similar consumable items, such as food. Although these items were previously unregulated, the new laws must be adhered to from the date they come into force. Although the organization has been in existence for some time, such a change is new to it, as it's never had to deal with something like this before. Referring to Figure 11, the following may be what is needed:

1. The new/changed law is a new/changed Business Arrangement. If the organization had a Business Arrangement system, the first step would be to record this new law there, including its date of effect.

2. As the new law applies to only a few select products, the next step would be to link it to the supplier contracts for those specific products. By doing this we can ascertain who the suppliers are for this product.

3. The next step is to follow the links from the Business Arrangement system to the Supplier, Supplies, and Supplies Ordering systems, to notify those suppliers of the changes required (if they weren't already aware of it), including any changes the organization requires in labeling and packaging. New or amended contracts may also need to be

negotiated with the suppliers and recorded in the Business Arrangement system.

4.  The Product system, as well as the Warehousing Inventory system, will then need to be checked to ascertain how much, and where existing stocks of these products are. Existing product that does not comply with the new law usually cannot be sold from the date of effect. Management will then need to decide how to deal with this old product (e.g., dispose of it or return it).

5.  If the suppliers can meet the new legal requirements, and the organization wishes to continue selling those products, new and compliant supplies will need to be ordered. This will need to be done through the Supplier, Supplies, and Supplies Ordering systems. When the new supplies arrive, they will need to be recorded in the Product system, as well as the Warehousing Inventory system.

This is an approximate guide in how our EA can be very quickly used to guide us in dealing with this kind of change. Experts in the retail sales area, who are more experienced in this type of business, may be able to provide more detail, as well as what other steps may be required.

## Time dimension

The major theme of this book has been about the organization and its environment, and how environmental factors impact the organization's internal systems. Change occurs in the environment and we have shown how to track those changes, which parts of the internal systems are affected by those changes, and to also look for the change vectors – the directions of change. Thus, we have discussed how to match attributes of external entities with similar, or the same, attributes of internal entities to track and allow for change, taking as simple examples the addresses or locations of customers with the address or location of the organization's store outlets. By doing this, we can arrive at an enterprise architecture which is both more robust and flexible in the face of change, as well as being more amenable to predict and adjust to the direction of change.

One aspect that we have yet to discuss is the time dimension. That is, how time affects the EA of an organization. As the old saying goes, time changes everything, but we are not suggesting that the EA is proof against changes over time. On the contrary, we need to try to consider the changes that time may make to our EA and incorporate methods to deal with changes over time. EA methodologies like DODAF emphasize an iterative approach to cover each business requirement, moving onto the next requirement with the next iteration, and perhaps iterating back over the same requirement to ascertain the effects of the passage of time on that requirement.

Another technique called entity life history (ELH) analyzes the start-to-end changes on key entities. For example, from the customer's first contact with the organization through to that customer no longer being a customer. The problems with ELH are firstly that it is a very much inside-out view, and secondly it usually looks at just one entity from the viewpoint of the organization. In this book, we have emphasized the outside-in view, the external environment, and how the organization's internal systems should be designed to cope with the environment.

Now we must examine how the environment, and especially our environmental entities, change over time, and how we can design an EA that will move with those changes. Time may change more than what we can ascertain through using the above methods like DODAF and ELH. To do this, we will look at some simple examples.

The first simple example comes from telecoms network engineering. A telecoms network is a series of nodes (such as switches and routers) connected by links.

When one node in the network, or the links running into it, has a fault it sets off an alarm, while the next node can also set off an alarm because it is not receiving stuff from the faulty node. Thus, you can get a series of alarms occurring in a chain, when only one node or link is really at fault. To trace which node/link is really at fault, network engineers use a technique called "root cause analysis" to determine which node/link is faulty and why.

In the terminology of this book, each alarm is an event, which needs to be responded to by one or more activities, for instance root cause analysis, or some other more immediate activities. However, telecoms network nodes are often re-configured by changing the links between the nodes. This in turn changes the network, which in turn changes the sequence of alarm events, possibly triggering a different set of activities in response. As previously discussed, activities (changing the network configuration) can trigger events or a series of events (alarms) which in turn may trigger activities (finding the root-cause fault), and events can trigger events in a chain of events. Thus the (alarm) events may change over time.

The second example involves products, like cars, changing hands. Initially the car is purchased new by customer A, and all warranties (Business Arrangements) and associated service products (like free servicing or roadside assist) are with customer A. Let's assume for this example that those warranties and associated products for the car are for a period of 5 years after purchase. However, after 2 years customer A sells the car to customer B. Would customer B therefore be entitled to expect that the warranties and associated service products continue with the car for the remainder of the initial period they were issued for (in this case a further 3 years)? The answer to this is usually "no," but may differ between manufacturers, even though the costs of these bundled warranties and services would have been included into the original price of the car. This could be because it is very difficult to track current ownership when the car changes hands.

Not tracking this change of ownership, then, may lead to later problems with compulsory recalls. The manufacturer simply does not know who the current owner of the vehicle is, and then relies on customer B seeing a public advertisement and bringing the vehicle back to a dealership to get the problem fixed. The costs of broadly advertising the recall may exceed the costs of keeping track of current ownership of their product plus direct notification to current owners. Thus, time has changed who the current customer for that product is.

The third example involves a product where the organization <u>must</u> keep track of who currently owns, or is the customer for, the product. The product is shares (equities) in the organization, which we discussed earlier as being both a Business Arrangement (evidence of part ownership in the organization), as well as being traded (bought and sold) like a Product. As a Product shares are priced at what the purchaser is prepared to pay for them. As a Business Arrangement, not only do shares evidence part ownership of the organization, but organizations pay dividends on them, and they may also incur government taxes such as on dividends or be treated as property for taxation purposes. As such, an organization with shares keeps records of who owns their shares, and those records are updated every time shares, as a Product, change hands over time.

It is therefore important that we consider the time dimension in our EA for the organization. In each of the three very simple examples discussed above we have seen that:

- Telecoms network configuration changes over time may change the order of alarm events.

- Car ownership changes over time may change warranties and associated service products.

- Shares changing ownership over time must be tracked.

# CHAPTER 6

# Implications of the New Approach

In the previous chapter we have seen how the components of our EA fit together, and how most mature larger organizations share similar business application systems. For smaller organizations, those functions done by application systems may be manually performed. We have also seen where the major differences lie, namely in the product manufacturing space and the warehousing space. This may give heart to commercial off-the-shelf (COTS) software companies, who provide some of these common application systems.

However, there is a catch: functionality required is not the same. For example, all organizations may need a customer system, but some organizations need a very function-rich and sophisticated system, while others can use a relatively simple system. Even if organizations share the same business application requirements, not all of them require the same range of functionality in those systems. Just like a cat, a dog, and a cow all have a liver, kidneys and a heart, the details of what those organs do and how they do it (functionality) may differ at the micro level.

What is it that distinguishes the functionality requirements of say, a customer system, between organization A and organization B? The answer goes right back to the beginning of this book: the different environments that those organizations need to operate in. Let us take as examples customer systems for two completely different types of organizations, namely a government social security department, which has pensions as one of its major products, and a large retail shop which sells electrical goods like washing machines and refrigerators.

The government social security department offers the pension product, which is paid to an individual, or couple as customers, who individually or combined, meet certain limits on their income and assets. Over the limit then customers cannot receive the age pension. In this case a customer system for this organization would need to:

- Hold *deep* information about its customers. This information would need to cover customers' assets, income, and whether they are living with another (existing or potential) customer.

- Be able to calculate pension entitlements based on very complex combinations of product features (e.g., pension rules) and the customers' deep information. This may be achieved through the product system itself.

- Be easily updated based on changing basic customer data.

The large retail shop sells a variety of products from different manufacturers out of its huge showroom. Customers and potential customers walk in and discuss their needs with sales people, who explain the functions of the goods, and help the customer make a choice of what item to buy. As part of the purchase process, the customer provides their name and address for product delivery and warranty purposes. In this case, a customer system for this organization would need to:

- Hold *shallow* information about the customer. This is limited to name, address, and contact details. This information should be easily and securely updated regularly.

- If a third-party product (such as delivery) is optioned in, the third party will need to be sent the necessary details (like delivery address).

In summary, we have considered two different organizations, both utilizing a customer system, but with vastly different depths of functionality and data holdings, due to different environmental factors in their products and customers. Again, these examples are certainly *not* cases where "one size fits all."

# Implications

Based on the above two examples and the discussion thus far in this book, there are a number of implications for:

- Organizations that **consume** business application systems

- Organizations that **supply** COTS business applications, and

- IT services companies that **develop** bespoke enterprise business applications for organizations.

We'll consider the implications for each of these classes of organizations in detail.

## Consumers of business applications

It may be stating the obvious that similar organizations with similar products operating in similar environments gravitate towards similar business application systems. A good example of this is in the telecoms industry, where similar (often identical) customer billing systems have been deployed by different companies for years. Buying the same or similar COTS products by similar organizations has both advantages and disadvantages. Although we won't analyze these here in any detail, the advantages usually center around a quick start and proven performance and technology, while the disadvantages usually center around being tied to the same or similar capabilities as your competitor organizations. Further down the track, organization A may wish to distinguish itself from organization B by offering different products, product packages, or targeting different customers, only to find that their hugely expensive COTS systems do not allow that to happen, or at least not without major surgery on them, which the vendor is unable or unwilling to carry out.

It is therefore important for EA practitioners to understand that although organization A and organization B may be competing in the same market with similar products and targeting similar customers, that does not mean that they operate in exactly the same environment. The reason for this is that for either A or B to succeed they must distinguish themselves in some respects, and this immediately means that the environments they operate in are different. That distinguishing may take the form of different products, product packages, product pricing, or different target customers. This is basic business behavior.

The EA for organization A and B may look identical, with both having customer systems, and customer billing systems, but A and B do not operate in exactly the same environment, and those systems must have different capabilities to allow them to be successful in their chosen environments. Architects must explore these issues with the organization. Often just asking questions about what the organization expects its environment (like products and customers) to be, will cause the organization to think through and clarify what environment it is aiming to operate in. Just having these conversations will often clarify both the organization's ideas and enterprise architects' understanding of the target environment. This in turn will assist in choosing a more relevant COTS product, or customizing one, or even specifying a purpose-built business application.

On the other hand, telecom A and telecom B may in fact quite successfully run the same or similar COTS accounting applications. The reason for this is that accounting products need to follow the same rules, regardless of the commercial organization using them, or what environment that organization operates in. Thus back-end business applications like accounting systems are not as subject to the general environment that the whole organization operates in, nor to changes in that environment. Those accounting rules form the specialist environment for the accounting systems, and that specialist accounting environment is the same or similar for most organizations.

In summary, it is the business applications which deal with the organization's environment, which need to be customized for that organization and that environment. Others, like back-end accounting systems, can be standard COTS products, which only need to follow the rules of accounting as applied in each country.

## Suppliers of COTS business applications

Commercial off-the-shelf (abbreviated *COTS*, also known as packages, or "shrink-wrapped software") business application systems have long been popular, for reasons including:

- Proven or known performance and functions

- Lower acquisition costs compared to bespoke development

- Generally lower risks to acquire, customize and install, as the vendor usually carries the bulk of the risk

- Perceived or reputational fit for purpose, and ready-made for installation (i.e. if it works for competitors, it should work for us).

It is important to understand the history or background that many COTS products share. Some products were developed as bespoke applications for an organization, and the developer, retaining the intellectual property rights (IPR) and code for the product, then proceeded to market the same product to different customers. Other products started off as basic systems with minimal functions, with the capability to have add-ons custom developed for each customer. These add-ons, where again the IPR was retained by the vendor, were then added to that product for its later customers.

As such, many of these COTS products were built for organizations which may not be operating in the same environment, or operate with the same rules, as the current potential customer for the product. It is important that this point is understood.

Therefore the suppliers of COTS business applications need to understand that organizations do operate in different environments, such that a customer system originally developed for a telecom organization may not necessarily be particularly useful for a retail chain selling electrical goods. Indeed, it may not be that useful for a telecom organization whose products and customer base differ greatly from the telecom for which the COTS product was developed.

This creates several implications for the suppliers of COTS business applications. These suppliers must understand the environments in which their potential customers operate. They must build flexibility into their COTS products, so that they can be tailored to different customers' environments. There must be an opportunity to build on or modify existing functions to suit different customers.

One other important factor, which we will discuss in more detail later in this chapter, is that of integration with other existing systems. A large portion of the effort of customizing COTS products is often spent in integrating it with other existing business applications within the customer's existing systems portfolio. That effort, and therefore the costs associated with it, could be substantially reduced if the most likely interfaces are identified, and provision made to cater for them, which could be through several mechanisms.

In summary, the "one size fits all" approach of COTS products suppliers is highly unlikely either to be true or to provide completely satisfactory business applications solutions for their customers. COTS suppliers need to be able to customize their products for each individual customer organization's environment, as well as their operating rules. COTS suppliers will also need to be able to integrate their products with other existing applications within the customer's existing IT environment.

## IT services companies

IT services companies provide a range of services, usually to organizational customers. These services can range from training through analyzing requirements and developing to those requirements, up to running of or supplying the customers' complete ICT requirements. Commonly a customer can express a business need or requirement for a business application system, and invite one or more IT services companies to provide a solution, whether that solution is a COTS product, or a bespoke development.

The problem for the IT services company then, becomes one of trying to understand the business, business environment, and context of the request from the customer or potential customer. Often IT services companies look at the customer's proposed solution without that understanding, take it literally, and proceed to propose a solution based on the supplied requirements.

The problem is often compounded by the customer's own solutions architects proposing incomplete technical solutions to a much wider business problem. The IT services company's personnel, lacking any in-depth understanding of the customer's business, simply follow the customer's suggested solution. This combination often ends up with unsatisfactory results for the customer.

The IT services company must understand the basics of the three-plus-one tier architecture and place the customer's proposed solution within that architecture. It then needs to understand the business environment that the customer must operate in. This will provide a head start to the IT services company. In fact, demonstrating that understanding by using it in their response to the customer's stated needs may even provide the IT services company with a distinct competitive advantage, all other things being equal.

As with the COTS product suppliers, IT services companies also need to give due consideration to integration of the customer's requested solution into the customer's existing portfolio of application systems. In fact, very often IT services companies will propose one or more COTS products, as part of their solution to the customer's stated requirements. They may also become involved with the integration effort for their solution with existing customer systems, or within their proposed solution. If the IT services company understands the customer's business environment, their existing applications systems portfolio, the positioning of the proposed solution, and its likely integration requirements, then they place themselves in a situation where they can really add value for their customer, and genuinely partner with their customer, to both parties' mutual benefit.

In summary, IT services companies can gain a serious competitive edge by researching and understanding their prospective customers' business environment, their existing suite of IT solutions, and the architectures discussed here, to become more successful in meeting their customers' needs. In fact, IT services companies are in a unique position to do that compared with COTS products suppliers.

# Integration

## A brief history

The seamless integration of data and functions across all an organization's IT portfolio has long been the holy grail of EA. In the previous chapter, the major integration pathways were indicated, although these are not all the required pathways.

In the 1970s, integration was thought of as purely at the data level, mainly through sharing of data between different business application systems. Initially files of data were transferred between application systems. Soon this method not only proved to be costly, but time consuming as well, because hundreds, if not thousands of files were regularly transferred between standalone business applications. Not only did the application supplying data need to download the requested data, but it needed to be formatted for the receiving application.

It was common for different business applications to request the same or similar data, in different formats. Then the receiving application had to upload that data and process it for its own use, all within strictly controlled time windows. The author knows of one exceptionally large organization which was spending approximately 40% of its total IT operational budget simply transferring files of data around different business applications.

When databases came into general use, one of their major selling points was that a single database could service more than one business application. This led to the idea that a single large corporate database supplying data to different systems, was the ideal solution, and early practitioners of EA tended to espouse this approach. This was underlined by the emergence of the enterprise data model (EDM) as the key to any self-respecting EA, and of course the corporate database was a natural implementation of the EDM. Unfortunately, EA theoreticians tended to be ahead of what the technology of the times could deliver, especially in terms of physical databases. There were other difficulties as well, especially as business agreement across the whole enterprise had to be obtained for every data field in its meaning, format, purpose, and validation rules. This was a huge undertaking.

The late 1980s and early 1990s saw the emergence of relational databases, and especially distributed relational databases, which made the "one big corporate database" idea somewhat more technically feasible, even if the "one database" was actually physically distributed across multiple servers. However, the one big corporate database still needed an enormous amount of analysis and design work to make it happen, and naturally precluded the use of COTS products, which are usually standalone islands of functionality and data.

As COTS products became more popular, especially for quick start-ups or replacements of ageing systems, EA practitioners had to go back to the drawing board in the search for the holy grail of integration. Around this time, the ideas of object-oriented methods started to make inroads into traditional approaches or methodologies around EA. At the same time there was a realization that simply integrating data was insufficient, and that process also needed to be integrated. So, a variety of technical solutions began to appear:

- **Screen scraping**. This referred to software that could read the input screens of another system, picking out the data entered there to use in its own processing. The advantage of this method was that the business user didn't need to enter the same data repeatedly into other systems.

- **Remote procedure calls and wrapper technology**. Remote procedure calls referred to software provided by one system to a second system, whereby the second system could call on selected functionality within the first system on a program-to-program basis. Wrapper technology was usually a third-party product provided to "wrap" one system and pass data to or from it, or call functionality within it, from another system.

- **Database links**. This referred to software provided within certain types of (usually relational) databases whereby selected data in one database could be viewed and even manipulated as if it were a native part of the second database.

Figure 12 illustrates the above three major types of these technologies. Unfortunately, these technical solutions had several drawbacks, including:

- The longer a business application is in use, the more some data fields diverge from their initial concept, definition, or validation. As an example, when they needed to collect additional information, business users often utilized a free-text or "comments" field.

- Database links (which allow one application to read or write directly to another application's database) can also cause problems. Rules about the data are often enacted within the application code, and direct access to that data by another application will bypass those rules, possibly leading to catastrophic results.

The main focus of the earlier history was point-to-point integration, such as simply getting two business applications to either exchange data, or one to do some processing for the other and return some answer. But what about point-to-multi-point integration, where one business application provided data or services to multiple other business applications? Given the drawbacks of using screen-scraping or database link technologies, the only effective method for integration was to use remote procedure calls between business applications. But remote procedure calls are point-to-point, not point-to-multi-point.

With the development and ubiquitous deployment of desktop computing, came the ideas of client-server, where the client was almost invariably the desktop, connected to the server, which was the business application running on a separate computer. The desktop client would handle the display tasks, while the server handled the business application processing and database tasks. The desktop also allowed business users to run multiple applications at the same time. However, this still left the problem of the server applications not communicating with each other.

Figure 12: Early attempts at integration between two business applications.

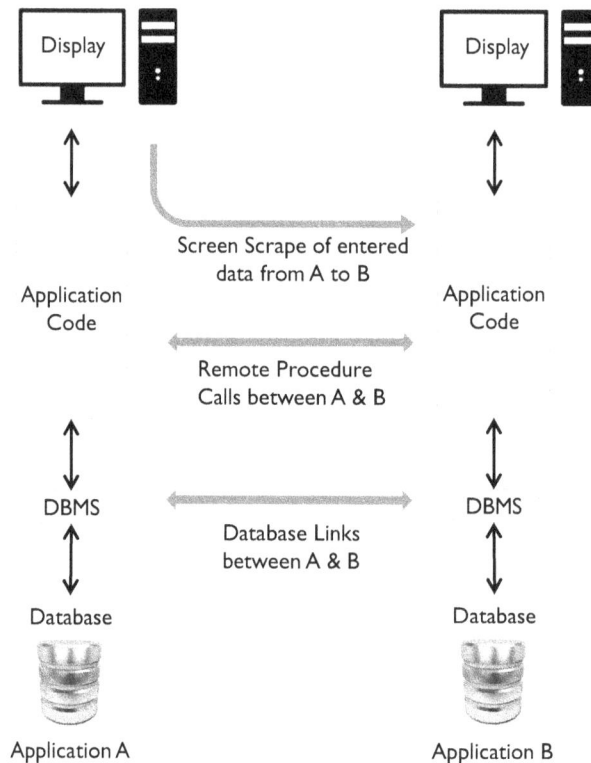

Almost in parallel with the development of the Internet came the development of enterprise integration software (EIS), often called middleware, which provided both the transport of data and requests for data, and traffic routing for these calls. A lot of work was done to make calls from one system to another independent of the system, as well as addressing issues of how one system could "talk" to multiple others and maintain the correct place in their "conversations," and security issues as well. The "single log on," where a caller did not need to repeatedly log into different applications, also became a central problem to solve.

With the rise of object-oriented methods and programming, came the development of the idea of "services" provided by one business application, which could be called by another or multiple business applications. The "provider" application would be connected to some kind of internal communications hub (like an intranet or EIS), and would receive remote calls from calling applications, given some input data, then return some output result – the service. Thus, the development of enterprise integration software, middleware, to provide transport for the calls to the service or multiple services, allowed the development of the ideas of Service-Oriented Architecture (SOA). The EIS also provides the ability for the "single log on," as well as other security services. SOA essentially provided the architectural and intellectual underpinning for EIS.

## Service Oriented Architecture

There is a lot of literature on service-oriented architecture (SOA). Essentially a *service* is a process of some sort, often encapsulating data, which is provided by the service *provider* to a service *consumer*, over some communications protocol or layer like the Web or EIS middleware. How a *service* is implemented is not known to the *consumer* (a black box). In many ways, a *service* is similar in concept to a program function like a square root function, within a programming language, but implemented across a network, between business applications.

In a SOA architecture, there are three important components, namely:

- A *service broker*, registry and/or repository. This component basically provides an index of available services to any requestor.

- A *service provider*. This component provides the service registered with the service broker, executes that service, and returns the results (if any) to the requestor. This may also include security services like the "single log on."

- A *service consumer* or *requestor*. This component locates the required service in the service broker and invokes the service.

It is important to note that the roles of service provider and service consumer can be changed. As such, a service provider, at the same time while providing the service, can be a consumer of other services (component services). It is unlikely (but not impossible) that, for the same service, the consumer-provider pair will interchange roles. However, the service broker will not change its role.

SOA is an enormously powerful and potent approach to the integration of business applications across the organization. However, SOA is not a magic bullet to fix integration issues, nor is it cheap or easy to implement. The reason is that it requires disciplined governance across the organization, and across the organization's IT portfolio. The organization needs to have a complete and agreed set of business services with definitions which are agreed to across the organization. Step by step, the precursors to a SOA implementation include, but are not confined to:

1. An enterprise data model (EDM) which defines organization data with agreed definitions across the organization. This forms the "common vocabulary" of the organization.

2. The EDM must then be mapped to existing application databases, using application data models, to identify where and how the underlying data is currently stored. Differences between the EDM definitions and those in the physical data storages need to be defined and documented.

3.  A set of agreed business services must then be developed, encapsulating the data from steps 1 and 2 into objects with defined behaviors. For this step, a methodology like Enterprise Object Modeling (EOM) can be quite useful. The Enterprise Object Model is the "common language" of the organization.

4.  Object behaviors (the "processing" part of data processing) then also need to be mapped to existing business applications.

5.  Once the business services are defined, these can be decomposed into component services at a finer granularity. Note that there is no reason why a component service can't also be used on its own.

Once the above tasks are completed, then implementation planning can begin. This may become complicated when the time factor is considered. For example, the replacement of an underlying legacy application when its replacement's functionality is still unknown, together with not knowing the timing of its retirement. Theoretically in this example, it shouldn't matter to the overall SOA implementation, providing the service(s) exposed and provided by the retiring legacy application are maintained by its replacement. Reality however means that this is not necessarily, or even commonly, the case.

In summary, SOA is an attractive option for integrating an organization's existing and future business application systems portfolio. However, it does require careful analysis, planning, and a disciplined approach to its execution, including over time. It is also certainly not a cheap option, given all the work that needs to be done to implement, as well as maintain it across the organization.

Given the importance of integrating business application systems across the organization, the cost of *not* doing so may exceed the costs of doing it. Thus, like any other major investment that an organization makes, a rational and realistic approach to investment in SOA needs to be taken. Earlier in this book we drew a parallel between living organisms such as a cat, and organizations. Organisms have methods of communication and integration of activities between different components (like nerve signals and chemical signals) within the organism. Thus SOA, as one of these methods, provides a parallel method of communication and integration of activities between different business application components within the organization. SOA is a conceptually elegant solution but should not be undertaken without a great deal of care.

However, implementing SOA, or a similar comprehensive real-time integration of business applications across the organization, is also likely to allow for some advanced technologies, such as artificial intelligence (AI) and/or expert systems (ES), to be introduced and deployed within the organization's IT portfolio.

## Artificial intelligence and expert systems in the EA

As with SOA, there exists much literature about Artificial Intelligence (AI) and Expert Systems (ES), which will not be repeated here. There are also a lot of news items about both AI and ES, and interest in these, especially AI, has been growing in recent years. This section looks at where some of these technologies are currently being used, and possible future applications of these technologies within the EA.

ES has been in use for over three decades and appears in several places. Most of these could be related to the "Manufacturing System" box discussed in Chapter 9. Both ES and AI have been deployed in manufacturing, usually in conjunction with robotics, in, for example, the manufacturing of motor vehicles.

ES/AI has also been successfully used as part of the "Manufacturing System" in banks and financial institutions, for applications such as assessing risks on various loan products. These often operate as an adjunct to larger business applications, such as workflow (activity management) engines. There are also numerous ES/AI components deployed to Business Intelligence suites, to make sense of huge volumes of data to present management with precise views of the operations of their organization.

ES/AI have been used increasingly for trolling through large holdings of unstructured data, to find what is relevant to the user search, and filtering out what is not. Searching through those large holdings (which are often based on fuzzy or imprecise search criteria) requires interpretation of the user's intent formulated in natural language, before performing the searches. The searches themselves must do more than simply matching keywords in large volumes of natural language texts. These kinds of applications are virtually impossible to do with an acceptable performance, without some form of ES/AI technology underpinning it.

Pioneering work is also being undertaken with ES/AI, often in conjunction with some form of robotics, to undertake everyday human tasks. One, possibly trivial example, is the humble household vacuum cleaner, being replaced by one that can be programmed to do all that work without destroying the contents of the household. Another more advanced example are automated piloting systems on passenger aircraft, which not only keep the aircraft on its course during cruising but can also help the pilot land and take off.

The present development of these technologies seems to point to two basic themes:

- Entirely replacing humans. This trend has been growing, and appears mainly in repetitive work, such as that required in manufacturing widgets (like cars parts).

- Supplementing or assisting humans. This trend can be seen in search engines, aircraft auto-pilots, and a range of other applications.

Attempts have been made in the past – and no doubt more will be made in the future – to entirely replace humans at the customer interface level.

So where does this current state of play leave our EA with respect to the deployment of ES/AI technologies? Predicting the future is so fraught that it will not be attempted here. Based on the above two trends, at the time of this book's publication, I see potential advancements to include:

- ES/AI technologies are more likely to be used within the middle layer of the three-plus-one organizational model (Product Development and Product Build).

- ES/AI technologies are also more likely to be used in the orthogonal Business Management layer, to help guide the organization's management.

- ES/AI technologies will continue being used in the bottom Suppliers and Supplies layer of the organization, especially in warehousing and JIT (just in time) approaches.

- ES/AI technologies could be used in the top Customers and Product Sales layer, assisting the organization's customer contact personnel with complex customer interactions.

The theme of this book has been that organizations are like organisms which have to survive, thrive, and deal with their environments which change, while their internal IT systems evolve to assist them to deal with that environment.

One possible idea for deployment of ES/AI technologies is described here. Just as organisms must monitor their environment for events which may affect them, so organizations must do the same.

Not all events necessarily or even immediately affect organizations, but often it is difficult to separate those which do or could, from those which are not especially relevant, especially if the volumes of events are very high. ES/AI technologies could perform this vital function. For example, vast numbers of events are recorded and reported on by news media, most of which have outlets for the "news" available on the Internet. Natural language ES/AI programs could be used to scan these news sources (in multiple languages), classed as events in this book, looking for items of interest and pertinent to the organization. Once found, the ES/AI programs could trigger activities such as "refer to manager X," including using another ES/AI SOA-based translation service, before presenting the article to "manager X."

Similar types of services could also be performed on other external entities such as Customers' feedback on social media about the organization's products, Products including competitors' products, Business Arrangements including new or changed laws and standards, Suppliers including their problems or adverse reports about their supplies. The list of possibilities is literally endless, and we will leave it to the reader to think of new and probably more original possible uses for ES/AI technologies in the organization's EA.

In summary, ES/AI technology is likely to become an important component of an organization's IT portfolio, and should therefore be carefully considered as part of the EA. One reason why this sub-section has been included here is that good integration between existing business applications should open major possibilities for deployment of ES/AI technologies.

# CHAPTER 7

# Non-Obvious Cases

Throughout this book we have discussed organizations, and the examples given have largely been commercial organizations. The new enterprise architecture applies to other types of organizations as well as commercial ones. However, it may not be obvious how it applies to some of these other types of organizations. In this chapter we will discuss and give some examples of these "non-obvious" cases.

In Chapter 2 we compared organizations to organisms. Both need to operate within their chosen environment, with the help of their internal organs for organisms, and their IT infrastructure for organizations. We also examined data, staying at the subject area level, which the IT portfolio of applications use, dividing those into internal and external data. Out of the eight subject areas, we identified five as being external and three as being internal.

Based on this, there are six key questions which EA practitioners need to ask, which initially will help define the environment that the organization operates in, and therefore drive the development of the EA it requires. These six questions are:

1.  What are your products?

2.  Who are your customers?

3. What are the business constraints, such as laws, agreements, contracts, and standards, under which you work?

4. Who are your suppliers?

5. What products do you obtain from them?

6. How does physical location affect your organization?

We will use these six questions to try to demonstrate that even non-obvious cases conform to the organizational models discussed in this book.

---

# Defense forces

A defense force is a military organization set up to protect and defend a nation. It usually consists of three or four major combat arms, plus supporting logistics. Depending on the nation the major combat arms are:

- Army, which is mainly responsible for land warfare
- Navy, which is mainly responsible for sea warfare
- Air force, which is mainly responsible for air warfare

For the purposes of this discussion, these arms will not be treated separately, as what applies in this discussion to one arm, should apply to all the arms. As such, the discussion will be at the defense force level.

The defense force is an organization which, as an arm of government, does not actually perform a service for the government until it is called into action by the government. In some ways, it can be considered an organization-in-waiting. Applying our six key questions to the defense force yields quite a bit of information, which is summarized immediately below, and then discussed in detail after.

1. **What are your products?** Defense force products are almost always services. We will call each act of service a "mission," which can consist of component products or services. Each mission is very much a tailored service product, defined specifically for the parameters of that particular security matter – just like the services provided by, say, a law firm.

2. **Who are your customers?** The government of the country is the only organization allowed to call the defense force into action; therefore they are its major customer. It could be argued that the whole population is the customer, but we will try to keep it simple here by naming the government. The government defines the mission product they require, and its desired outcomes, objectives, and goals.

3. **What are the business constraints, such as laws, agreements, contracts, and standards, under which you work?** These include laws of the defense force's own country, defense treaties with other countries, international agreements and obligations, and standards of behavior.

4. **Who are your suppliers?** Suppliers to the defense force consist of two groups – those that supply the resources used by the force, and those that supply the consumable resources. Like many business organizations, suppliers provide the logistics that a defense force requires to carry out its mission.

5. **What products do you obtain from them?** Supplies to the defense force include everything from capital equipment it uses as resources (including capital equipment like planes, tanks, and guns), through all the consumables it requires to sustain its operations (including food and ammunition).

6.  **How does physical location affect your organization?** Physical location is extremely pertinent to a defense force; it affects nearly every logistical aspect of the mission.

Defense forces also talk in terms of capabilities, which are those standard service products it *could* provide with the resources it possesses. One example of a capability is the ability to land paratroopers in a specific area. Thus, a capability (or a group of capabilities) could be considered a standard product component, to be used as necessary, within the service product of the overall mission.

Examining each of the six answers, we can predict which systems are most likely to be required:

**Customers and Product Sales**

- **Customer System**. Unlikely, as there is really only one customer: the government of the day

- **Customer Billing System**. Not needed

- **Product System**. Yes, to put together standard component products for the overall mission; this is analogous to a planning system

- **Order System**. Not needed

- **Event System**. Almost certainly, to track events of interest which may have direct or indirect impacts on the mission

**Product Development and Product Build**

- **Business Arrangements System**. Almost certainly needed

- **Activity System**. Almost certainly needed; it may be tied to the Product System

- **Resources System**. Yes

- **Employees System**. Yes

- **Manufacturing System**. In this case, since the product is the given mission, the "manufacturing system" is more like a "training system," enabling the defense agency to complete its mission as promised (i.e. deliver its product)

**Suppliers and Supplies** (commonly termed "logistics")
- **Supplies System**. Yes; may include information

- **Supplier System**. Yes

- **Supplies Ordering System**. Yes

- **Supplier Accounts System**. Yes

- **Warehousing Inventory System**. Yes

**Business Management**
- **Payroll System**. Yes

- **General Ledger**. Yes, including subsidiary systems of Accounts Payable, Accounts Receivable, and Assets

- **Business Intelligence**. Yes, and probably on a wider and more comprehensive scale than most other organizations

Defense forces, by providing tailored service products to their customer, the government of the country, therefore fits the standard model that has been outlined in this book. See next sub-section for the discussion of the civilian portion of a government's defense portfolio.

## Government departments and agencies

Government departments and agencies perform a range of different functions, so any discussion as brief as this one, will need to be very general. However, we can still ask the same six key questions and infer some general answers.

1. **What are your products?** These are many and varied, depending on the department or agency. Service products, such as advice to the government of the day, are probably common across all departments and agencies. Other service products, such as collecting revenues, or enforcing laws, are also common for many agencies and departments. Managing the delivery of infrastructure projects, as well as services to the public in the health care (hospitals), education, transport and transport infrastructure are also common products. Another large set of products involve social security products, provided to sections of the population by some departments and agencies. There is also the support of defense forces in terms of logistics and veterans' welfare.

2. **Who are your customers?** The customers of government departments and agencies range from the government itself (for the service products of advice, collecting revenues, and law enforcement), to recipients of government products, such as pensioners and patients in government-run hospitals.

3. **What are the business constraints such as laws, agreements, contracts, and standards, under which you work?** These are too numerous to mention here, as all government departments and agencies operate under enabling legislation. There are some laws which pertain specifically to one department or agency, and some laws which pertain to more than one. Some laws/regulations also define the products that departments or agencies must provide, as well as possibly the customers to whom those products are provided.

4. **Who are your suppliers?** Suppliers may be individuals or organizations, and may range from those who supply information and money (like taxpayers) to those that supply widgets and services. There are also classes of suppliers who may be totally unknown or anonymous, especially those supplying certain types of data or information products.

5. **What products/supplies do you obtain from them?** Supplies may include information, money (e.g., taxes), or physical things like paperclips and computers. It should be noted that information or raw data form a large portion of supplies that governments seek. Indeed, some departments and agencies do nothing else than collect raw data and transform this into information products for their customers, who can be the government, or can be other departments or agencies, or persons, or organizations outside the government sector.

6. **How does physical location affect your organization?** Physical location is usually of lesser importance to government departments or agencies, except as outlets for their products such as social security offices, electoral boundaries and polling stations, and embassies in foreign countries. Physical location is of importance when infrastructure projects are being contemplated.

In terms of systems likely to be required, these are so dependent on the individual department or agency that it's impractical to make a list. For example, a social security department that deals with thousands of pensioners will need a customer system, while a treasury department, which only has a few customers, may not. Both probably will need a product system.

Most government departments and agencies provide service type products to their customers. Some provide financial products. Some actually provide widgets (physical things) as products, such as books and publications, number plates, labels, and medical stuff like drugs and bandages.

However, some government agencies are actually business enterprises, such as the postal service, and should be treated as such by EA practitioners, whether they make profits or not.

---

# Non-commercial organizations

There are some types of organizations which are neither governmental nor commercial. Some of these are labelled "not for profit" organizations, but there are also non-commercial organizations which do run for profit. Examples of non-commercial organizations (whether they run for profit or not) include:

- **Charitable organizations**. These generally seek donations of funds to use in assisting individuals in need, like the homeless or unemployed.

- **Clubs, including sporting clubs**. These are generally organizations set up for the benefit of their membership, generally in pursuit of some common interest such as a sport, or vintage cars. However, it must be noted that in professional sports, sporting clubs are in fact businesses, and run as such. These are excluded from discussions here, as the focus is on non-professional non-business activities.

- **Support organizations**. These exist to support some other activity, usually one that is also non-profit. One example of this is a support organization which raises money for ancillary equipment for a rural fire service. The fire service is comprised of mainly volunteer fire fighters, and receives most of its equipment from the government, but the support organization supplies what the government does not. Support organizations are also commonly known as *auxiliaries*.

Rather than stepping through each of the six questions for each example of these organizations, we will summarize some possible answers relevant to many different examples.

**Charitable organizations**

- Products are goods and services to individuals. The goods may be donated or purchased items. Services can range from medical services through building services to care services. A well-organized charity should have a product system.

- Customers are almost exclusively individuals. A well-organized charity should have a customer system, to keep track of who they helped, and perhaps for follow-up to that assistance.

- Charitable organizations often operate under special legal provisions, which allows them to collect money from donors, as well as perhaps operating under special legal and other arrangements in providing products to their customers. In some cases, these organizations also operate in areas where standard government-controlled legal frameworks may be absent, and non-government frameworks apply. It would be of some advantage for such charitable organizations to record and track all these frameworks by utilizing a business arrangements system.

- Suppliers to charitable organizations consist of those who provide the financial support needed to operate and make the products, and parts of the products such as equipment for water purification. Suppliers may also be people who provide voluntary services to or through the charitable organization.

- Supplies to charitable organizations consist of financial support, and mainly widgets to be provided to its customers. Service supplies may also be provided in shape of voluntary services provided by people.

- Location is usually of importance to charitable organizations, as this determines where they deliver their products to their customers.

## Clubs, including sporting clubs

- Products are mainly services, but can also be goods, premises, and land for individual customers. For example, sporting clubs provide a range of products including sporting goods, and grounds to play the sport on, as well as services in the club house and coaching in the sport by professional or amateur coaches. For other clubs, services could be accommodation and/or hospitality (restaurant) products.

- Clubs are distinguished by the fact that all their members are customers, but not all customers are members. A well-organized club should have a customer system, perhaps called a member system.

- Clubs are generally treated under the law as incorporated bodies, and thus are little different from business organizations. As such, they will also have an employer-employee relationship with those personnel who work for the club (including, for professional sports, the contracted players). Clubs commonly also have a set of club rules which apply internally to their members and/or employees only. A business arrangement system could be of benefit to some clubs.

- Suppliers to clubs are like suppliers to any other business, ranging from equipment suppliers to food and beverage suppliers, as well as suppliers of services (such as specialist coaching and medical services). Suppliers to clubs may also be sponsors; in return for advertisement, they supply the club with funds.

- Supplies to clubs are likely to be standard for the type of business, like food, beverages, and sporting equipment. A supplies system could be of benefit to larger clubs.

- Location is unlikely to be of great importance for clubs, except that some sporting clubs have recruiting areas allocated to them.

## Support organizations

These types of organizations often closely resemble charitable organizations and are often run in a similar way. Thus, their answers to the six questions are likely to be similar to those of the charitable organizations.

We have tried to show through the above examples that even organizations far removed from commercial businesses can benefit from the new EA. This is mainly because these organizations still share the same characteristics as those commercial organizations, namely:

- The three-plus-one model applies to them

- They have products (services or widgets) which they provide to their customers

- They have customers for their products, even if those products are given away free

- They have suppliers and supplies

- They have a set of business arrangements which apply to them, and/or standards with which they must comply

The conclusion to draw from this is that the models described in this book apply to all organizations. Thus, the enterprise architecture approach described in this book can be used with every type of organization.

# CHAPTER 8

# Closing Summary

In this book we have defined and described a number of key concepts, including the following cornerstones:

- An organization operates within its chosen environment, and EA must support its operations in that environment.

- Changes to the environment impact its EA. As such, the EA must be flexible enough to adapt.

The process of developing the EA can be a lengthy and costly exercise, and thus the EA should not be left on the shelf to gather dust. An EA's primary purpose is to provide the organization, which invests in it, with a roadmap to the future of a significant investment in information processing, storage, and management that is the organization's IT portfolio. This map, as a reminder, must include three major characteristics:

- We must be able to use it to plan our trip. We use it to see where all the objects of interest for our journey are, how to get there, which roads or directions to travel, and the distances and likely travel times for our journey.

- The map must also show the impact of any change. Thus, for example, if we learn of a major road accident blocking a road that we planned to take up ahead, we must be able to consult our map, rapidly evaluate the impact of that blockage on our travel plans, and work out any possible alternative routes.

- Maps also must be able to be updated, just like our EA needs to be updated with changes in the environment. Even a regular old road map is not static, as roads are moved and renamed.

When used to examine the impact of some change, it's often the case that a rapid overall picture of the change is required, and thus a map without too much detail is often more useful than a highly detailed map, at least in the first instance. Once the broad scope of the change is appreciated, and an overall response devised, then we can delve into the detail.

This book presents key concepts at a "big picture" scale, granting a high-level understanding of the organization and its environment for the EA. We will now return to some of these key concepts, to summarize these essential ideas discussed in detail throughout this book.

## Data subject areas

In Chapter 4 we discussed data subject areas. We showed that there were eight data subject areas, which contain all structured data within an EA.

Key concepts include:

- A data subject area is a grouping of a detailed data model of a common subject. Thus, the Product data subject area contains a detailed model of the data surrounding the organization's products.

- A detailed data model of a subject has links or relationships with other subjects, also at the detailed level. There may be many such links.

- In the data subject area diagram, we show only one link between each pair of subject areas. Each of those single links represents all the links in the more detailed models. Multiple relationships between the detailed models of Activity and Event are all represented by just one line between the Activity and the Event subject areas.

- Each subject area has links to other subject areas, but not necessarily to all subject areas.

- Regardless of the differences in the detailed data models between different types of organizations contained in each subject area, all organizations have the same eight subject areas.

- There are seven subject areas that contain original data.

- There is one subject area that contains derived data – the Derived Object subject area. This subject area is of crucial importance to "back office" functions, such as the accounts function, and to business management.

- The data entities which form the detailed data model for the Derived Object subject area, are traceable to one or more data entities in the other seven subject areas of original data. Thus, every derived object is traceable to and from original "real" data in those seven subject areas.

Of great importance was the Subject Area model shown earlier and reproduced here for convenience:

Figure 13. Standard data Subject Area model for organizations.

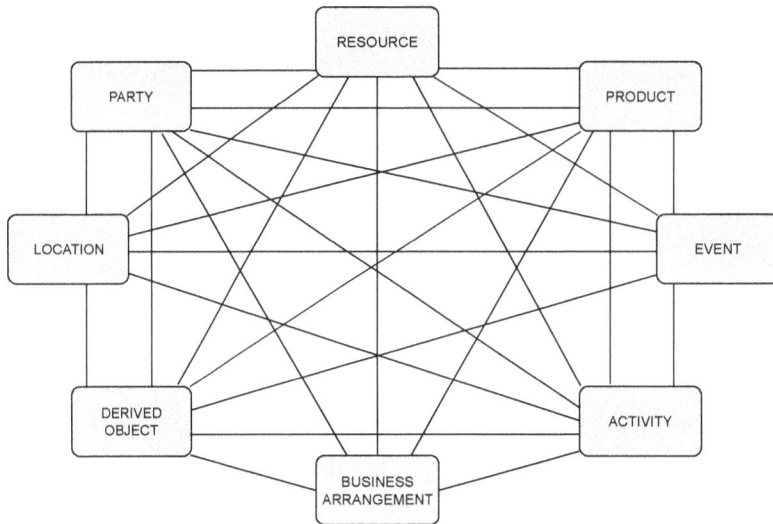

---

## Internal and external subject areas

Following the data subject areas, we introduced the idea that some subject areas are mainly internal. Others are external to the organization, and some are both internal and external. We'll briefly describe these below.

External Subject Areas include:

- **Party**. This usually refers to Customers and Suppliers, although it could include others. The Party subject area is both internal and external, depending on the role played by the Party (i.e. customer is external, while employee is internal, although the same Party could play both roles). We have chosen to depict it as external because of the importance of external parties within the environment of the organization. Party has two main subtypes called organization and person, although sometimes a third subtype called work group is added.

- **Product**. Although produced internally, this is offered externally, and provides the organization's main interaction with its environment, through its customers for those products. Product can also include competitors' products. As such, Product is treated as external.

- **Event**. These are things that happen outside of the control of the organization, and to which the organization needs to respond with one or more activities. One example of a common event was a customer order for a product.

- **Business Arrangement**. These things govern the organization's behavior. Examples included laws, contracts with other organizations, and standards. Although some business arrangements can be internal like management instructions, many of these internal business arrangements are manifested as business rules and process (activity) flows. Some business arrangements, like customer accounts or supplier contracts, are both internal and external, but we treat these as external.

- **Location**. This is a geographic place in three-dimensional space.

Internal Subject Areas include:

- **Resource**. This includes all those things that the organization uses to conduct its business and produce its products. It specifically excludes people.

- **Activity**. These are the actions carried out within the organization, either by people or computers. A linked set of activities is a process.

- **Derived Object**. As mentioned above, these are derivations of data in the other seven subject areas.

# Three-plus-one level organization model

In Chapter 3 we introduced the idea that all organizations share a similar structure of three horizontal layers or tiers, plus one orthogonal vertical business management layer or tier. Some, usually extremely large, complex organizations also organize themselves into vertical "silos', commonly for major groups of products in each silo, with the silos being multiples of the basic three-plus-one structure, and an over-arching business management layer. There can be many variations on this, and readers may know of some which were not mentioned here. However, the basic principles remain the same, so we stuck with our simpler "three-plus-one" structure for the purposes of this book and this summary. We developed these ideas using the three-plus-one model, gradually evolving that model into the picture which is repeated below.

Figure 14. Common Systems Architecture and Subject Areas.

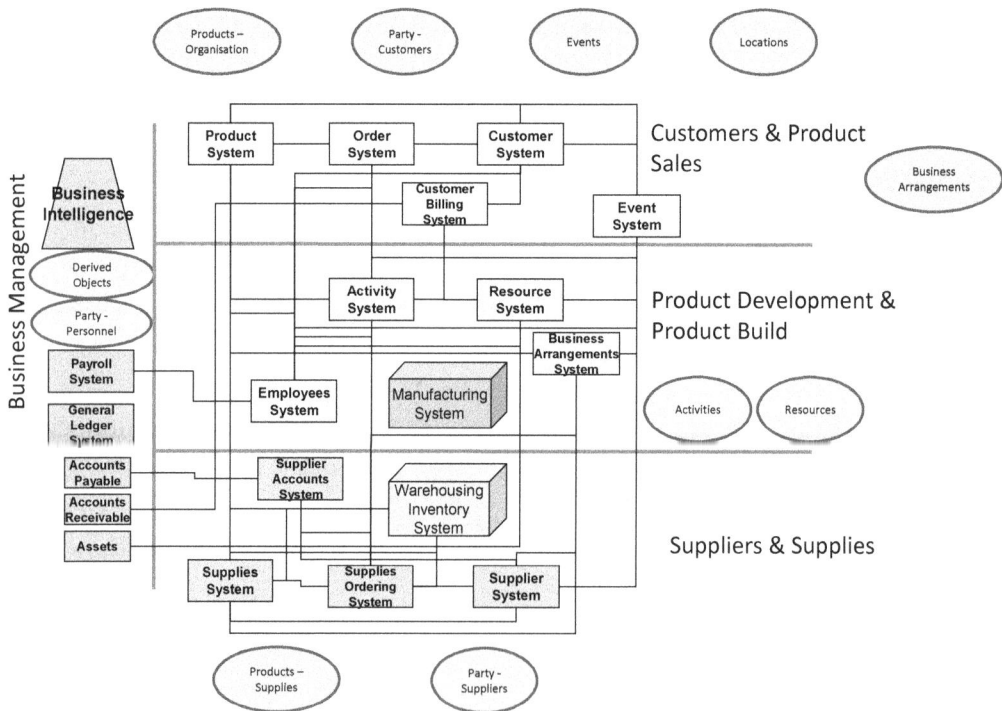

# Dealing with change

As discussed earlier in this book, change may come in many forms, so trying to categorize or describe all types of change would be futile. However, just like the example of the high-level limited-detail map, we can use our new EA to rapidly determine the impacts of changes in the organization's environment on its internal systems and processes.

We do this through links between internal and external entities within the corresponding data subject areas. Also as discussed earlier, those links are through attributes of internal and external entities, and come in two forms:

- **Overt relationships**. These are direct relationships, using linking attributes called foreign keys. One example provided was of the external entity Event, which has a direct relationship with the internal entity Activity, such that most commonly we have "Event *triggers* Activity". In this form, a new instance of Event, would require one or more new Activity instances to be developed.

- **Common value relationships**. These are more subtle, but just as important, as the links are expressed through sharing common values for attributes of the corresponding internal and external entities. One example we gave was where the value of the attribute *address* for a customer (Party in the role of customer – an external entity), changed from the value of the same attribute for the organization, such that this change impacted on the sale of the organization's products to this customer.

With the above in mind, and with our new EA, we can be reasonably confident of dealing with impacts of changes in the organization's environment.

In the opening chapters it was stated categorically that this book is not about how to do enterprise architecture. That has been well covered in numerous other approaches and methodologies. Nor is this book intended to replace the detailed work required by those approaches and methodologies to deliver a complete EA for any organization. What this book is intended to do is add a new perspective, and through that, add value to the Enterprise Architecture that is delivered to organizations.

# Index

www.ingramcontent.com/pod-product-compliance
Lightning Source LLC
Chambersburg PA
CBHW081525220326
41598CB00036B/6334